IMAGINING SHAKESPEARE

# Imagining Shakespeare

## A History of Texts and Visions

STEPHEN ORGEL

palgrave
macmillan

First published 2003 by
PALGRAVE MACMILLAN
Houndmills, Basingstoke, Hampshire RG21 6XS and
175 Fifth Avenue, New York, N.Y. 10010
Companies and representatives throughout the world

PALGRAVE MACMILLAN is the global academic imprint of the Palgrave
Macmillan division of St Martin's Press LLC and of Palgrave Macmillan Ltd.
Macmillan® is a registered trademark in the United States, United Kingdom
and other countries. Palgrave is a registered trademark in the European Union
and other countries.

ISBN 1–4039–1177–0

This book is printed on paper suitable for recycling and
made from fully managed and sustained forest sources.

A catalogue record for this book is available
from the British Library.

A catalogue record for this book is available
from the Library of Congress

10   9   8   7   6   5   4   3   2   1
12   11   10   09   08   07   06   05   04   03

Printed and bound in Great Britain by
Antony Rowe Ltd, Chippenham and Eastbourne

For Terry Castle

# Contents

*List of Figures and Plates*                                                    viii
*Preface and Acknowledgments*                                                    xiv

1   Imagining Shakespeare                                                          1

2   Staging Clio                                                                  38

3   History and Biography                                                         65

4   Magic and History                                                            85

5   The Pornographic Ideal                                                       112

6   Imagining Shylock                                                            144

7   Epilogue                                                                     163

*Notes*                                                                          164
*Index*                                                                          168

# List of Figures and Plates

## Figures

1.1   *Measure for Measure* II.2 from the Padua folio. Reproduced by
      courtesy of the University of Virginia Press.                            7
1.2   The performance of *Edipo Tiranno* (*Oedipus Rex*) at the opening of
      the Teatro Olimpico in Vicenza, 1585. From a fresco in the theater.    10
1.3   Arend van Buchel after Johannes de Witt, the Swan Playhouse,
      London, c. 1595. University Library, Utrecht, ms. 842 fol. 132r.       11
1.4   *Arden of Feversham* (1633), woodcut illustration on the verso of
      the title page. Huntington Library.                                    12
1.5   Thomas Kyd, *The Spanish Tragedy* (1615), woodcut from the
      title page. By permission of the Folger Shakespeare Library.           13
1.6   Henry Peacham (?), c. 1595, a scene from *Titus Andronicus*.
      Longleat Portland Papers I f. 159v. By kind permission of
      the Marquess of Bath, Longleat House.                                  14
1.7   Sebastiano Serlio, The Tragic Scene, from *Architettura*, 1545.        16
1.8   Sebastiano Serlio, The Comic Scene, from *Architettura*, 1545.         17
1.9   Sebastiano Serlio, The Satiric or Pastoral Scene, from
      *Architettura*, 1545.                                                  18
1.10  Inigo Jones, setting for the Sieur de Racan's *Artenice* at
      Whitehall, 1626. Devonshire Collection, Chatsworth.
      Reproduced by permission of the Duke of Devonshire and
      the Chatsworth Settlement Trustees.                                    20
1.11  Title page to Ben Jonson's *Workes*, 1616, engraved by William Hole.   22
1.12  Thespis in his cart, detail of 1.11.                                   23
1.13  Choric dance, detail of 1.11.                                          23
1.14  Frontispiece to *Julius Caesar* in Nicholas Rowe's edition of
      Shakespeare, 1709.                                                     25
1.15  Frontispiece to *Volpone* in Tonson's edition of Ben Jonson, 1716.     26

1.16    Frontispiece to *As You Like It* in Nicholas Rowe's edition of
        Shakespeare, 1709.                                                        27
1.17    Giovanni Battista Guarini, *Il Pastor Fido*, 1602, frontispiece to Act 3.    28
1.18    After Robert Smirke, The Lover, from The Seven Ages of Man
        in *As You Like It*. From Boydell's *Prints...Illustrating the Dramatic Works
        of Shakespeare*, 1803. Stanford University Library.                       29
1.19    Richard Tarlton, wood engraving after a contemporary
        drawing, from *Tarleton's Jests*, ed. J. O. Halliwell (London, 1844).    31
1.20    Robert Armin, *The History of the Two Maids of More-clacke*, 1609,
        title page. Huntington Library.                                          32
1.21    Portrait of Edward Alleyn (British school). Reproduced by
        permission of the Trustees of Dulwich College Picture Gallery.           33
1.22    Faustus conjuring, from the title page of *Doctor Faustus*, 1620.
        British Library.                                                         34
1.23    John Green as Nobody in the play *Nobody and Somebody*.
        Watercolour drawing. Stiftsarchiv Rein.                                  35
1.24    After Nathaniel Dance, *Garrick as Richard III*. Stanford
        University Library.                                                      36
2.1/2.2 Ellen Tree (Mrs Charles Kean) as the Chorus in *Henry V*.
        Watercolor. By permission of the Folger Shakespeare Library.          39/40
2.3     Frontispiece to *Henry VIII* in Rowe's Shakespeare, 1709.              44
2.4     Spranger Barry and Isabella Nossiter in *Romeo and Juliet*, 1759.
        Engraving after a painting by R. Pyle.                                   46
2.5     Romeo and Juliet, picture postcard *c*. 1975.
        Edizzioni G. Randazzo, Verona.                                           47
2.6     Garrick as Hamlet. Mezzotint after a painting by Benjamin Wilson.
        Stanford University Library.                                            48
2.7     John Philip Kemble as Hamlet, Covent Garden, 1783.
        Stanford University Library.                                            49
2.8     Frontispiece to *Coriolanus* from Rowe's Shakespeare, 1709.            52
2.9     James Quin as Coriolanus. By permission of the Folger
        Shakespeare Library.                                                     53
2.10    Garrick in William Whitehead's *The Roman Father*. From *The Universal
        Magazine*, February 1750.
        By permission of the Folger Shakespeare Library.                         54
2.11    *Coriolanus*, engraving after Nicholas Poussin. Copyright
        British Museum.                                                          55
2.12    J. R. Planché, royal effigies from the reigns of Henry II,
        Richard I and King John, from his *History of British Costume*, 1847.    55
2.13    Eugène Delacroix, The Bedchamber Scene in *Hamlet*,
        lithograph (1844).                                                       57
2.14    Setting for Charles Kean's *Macbeth*, Princess's Theatre, 1853.
        Victoria and Albert Museum.                                             58
2.15    Charles and Ellen Kean as Macbeth and Lady Macbeth, 1853.
        Photo, Victoria and Albert Museum.                                       59
2.16    Daniel Maclise, the Play Scene from *Hamlet*. Print after the painting.    60

2.17    Edwin A. Abbey, the Play Scene from *Hamlet*. Yale University
        Art Gallery, Edwin Austin Abbey Memorial Foundation.                60
2.18    Henry Irving as Macbeth, 1888. Drawing by
        J. Bernard Partridge, from Ellen Terry, *The Story of My Life*, 1906.    61
2.19    John Singer Sargent, Ellen Terry as Lady Macbeth. Grisaille.
        By courtesy of the National Portrait Gallery, London.               62
2.20    Edward Gordon Craig, King Lear in the Storm. Woodcut.               63
3.1a/b  Title page opening of the First Folio. Courtesy of the Master
        and Fellows of Trinity College, Cambridge, and of the Pelican
        Shakespeare.                                                     66/67
3.2     George Chapman, from *The Whole Works of Homer, Prince of Poetts*,
        1616. By permission of the Folger Shakespeare Library.              69
3.3     Ben Jonson, from the second edition of the *Works*, 1640.            70
3.4     The funeral monument to Shakespeare, Holy Trinity Church,
        Stratford-Upon-Avon. Courtesy of Holy Trinity Church.               71
3.5     The Chandos Portrait. By courtesy of the National Portrait
        Gallery, London.                                                    72
3.6     The Chesterfield Portrait, *c.* 1660–70, attributed to Pieter Borseller.
        By permission of the Shakespeare Birthplace Trust,
        Stratford-Upon-Avon.                                                73
3.7     The Soest Portrait, *c.* 1660–80, attributed to Gerard Soest.
        By permission of the Shakespeare Birthplace Trust,
        Stratford-Upon-Avon.                                                74
3.8     Louis Roubiliac, Shakespeare. By permission of the Folger
        Shakespeare Library.                                                75
3.9     James Sant, *Shakespeare as a Boy of Twelve*. Whereabouts unknown.   76
3.10    Engraving after Hogarth, *Garrick as Richard III* (detail).          79
3.11    Frontispiece to Bell's Shakespeare, 1774.                            80
3.12    John Mortimer, The Poet. By permission of the Folger
        Shakespeare Library.                                                81
3.13    The Shakespeare Death Mask. City of Darmstadt, Germany.             82
4.1     A seventeenth-century Puck. The volume first appeared in
        1624. By permission of the Folger Shakespeare Library.              88
4.2     Detail of a memorial engraving by Francis Delarem (*c.* 1617)
        of Queen Elizabeth wearing a crescent moon in her hair.
        The figure is based on a Hilliard miniature.                       90
4.3     Frontispiece to *A Midsummer Night's Dream* in Nicholas Rowe's
        Shakespeare, 1709.                                                  91
4.4     Henry Fuseli, Titania and Bottom. Engraving by G. Rhodes
        after Henry Fuseli's painting for Woodmason's Shakespeare Gallery,
        1793–94. Stanford University Library.                              93
4.5     Henry Fuseli, Titania, Bottom and Oberon. From Boydell's
        *Prints...Illustrating the Dramatic Works of Shakespeare*, 1803.
        Stanford University Library.                                        96

4.6    Crispin van de Passe, memorial portrait of Elizabeth as Iustitia.
       By permission of the Folger Shakespeare Library.                        99
4.7    The interrogation of witches, from James Carmichel,
       *Newes from Scotland declaring the Damnable Life and death of Doctor Fian.*
       Bodleian Library, University of Oxford; Douce F210.                     100
4.8    Fian and the cow, above; Fian riding behind the devil on a
       black horse, below. Bodleian Library, University of Oxford;
       Douce F210.                                                             102
4.9    The devil directs the activities of witches. Note the sinking ship at
       the upper left. Bodleian Library, University of Oxford; Douce F210.     103
4.10   Inigo Jones, costume for Lucy, Countess of Bedford as
       Penthesilea in *The Masque of Queens*, 1609. Devonshire
       Collection, Chatsworth. Reproduced by permission of the
       Duke of Devonshire and the Chatsworth Settlement Trustees.              106
4.11   Inigo Jones, costume for Henry, Prince of Wales, in the title
       role in *Oberon*, 1611. Devonshire Collection, Chatsworth.
       Reproduced by permission of the Duke of Devonshire and
       the Chatsworth Settlement Trustees.                                     107
4.12   Inigo Jones, dancing satyrs, probably not related to *Oberon*.
       Devonshire Collection, Chatsworth. Reproduced by
       permission of the Duke of Devonshire and the Chatsworth
       Settlement Trustees.                                                    108
4.13   Inigo Jones, fairies in *Oberon*. Devonshire Collection, Chatsworth.
       Reproduced by permission of the Duke of Devonshire and the
       Chatsworth Settlement Trustees.                                         109
4.14   William Hole, Prince Henry at the Lance, dedicatory
       engraving from Michael Drayton's *Poly-Oibion*, 1613.                   110
5.1    Marcantonio Raimondi, engraving after Giulio Romano, I *Modi*,
       first position. Paris, Bibliothèque Nationale de France. Ae 52,
       don 3976.                                                               113
5.2    Marcantonio Raimondi, engraving after Giulio Romano, I *Modi*,
       eleventh position. Vienna, Albertina, Wien, inv. It. I 22, p. 49.       113
5.3    I *Modi*, woodcut 1. Private Collection.                                114
5.4    I *Modi*, woodcut 2. Private Collection.                               115
5.5/5.6 I *Modi*, woodcuts 10 and 16. Private Collection.                 116/117
5.7    I *Modi*, woodcut 3. Private Collection.                               118
5.8    I *Modi*, woodcut 9. Private Collection.                               119
5.9    Giulio Romano, Apollo in his Chariot. Ceiling fresco in the
       Palazzo Tè, Mantua. Copyright Scala/ Art Resource New York.            120
5.10   Giulio Romano, Cupid and Psyche bathing. Fresco in the
       Palazzo Tè, Mantua. Copyright Scala/ Art Resource New York.            124
5.11   Frontispiece to *The Winter's Tale* from Nicholas Rowe's
       Shakespeare, 1709.                                                      128
5.12   Hannah Pritchard as Hermione in Garrick's *Florizel and Perdita*.
       Engraving after a lost painting by R. E. Pine, *c.* 1760.
       By permission of the Folger Shakespeare Library.                        129

5.13    Elizabeth Farren as Hermione, *c.* 1780. Engraving after a
        painting by Johann Zoffany. Birmingham Shakespeare Library.      130
5.14    Elizabeth Hartley as Hermione, *c.* 1780. From *The Westminster
        Magazine*. By permission of the Shakespeare Centre Library.      131
5.15    I. Dayes, setting for the opening scene of Charles Kean's
        production of *The Winter's Tale*, 1856. Victoria and Albert Museum.   132
5.16    I. Dayes, design for the statue scene in Kean's *Winter's Tale*,
        1856. Birmingham Shakespeare Library.                            133
5.17    C. R. Leslie, Mrs Charles Kean as Hermione in *The Winter's Tale*.
        Royal Shakespeare Theatre Picture Gallery,
        Stratford-Upon-Avon.                                             134
5.18    Ellen Terry as Mamillius and Charles Kean as Leontes, 1856.
        Photograph. By permission of the Shakespeare Centre Library.     135
5.19    Ellen Tree (Mrs Charles Kean) as Hermione, 1856.
        Photograph. By permission of the Shakespeare Centre Library.     136
5.20    Ellen Terry as Hermione, His Majesty's Theatre, 1906.
        Photograph. By permission of the Shakespeare Centre Library.     137
5.21    Mary Anderson as Hermione, Lyceum, 1887. Photograph.
        By permission of the Folger Shakespeare Library.                 138
5.22    Mary Anderson as Perdita, Lyceum, 1887. Photograph.
        By permission of the Folger Shakespeare Library.                 139
5.23    Albert Rutherston (i.e., Rothenstein), costume design for
        Hermione in *The Winter's Tale*, Savoy Theatre, 1912. From Albert
        Rutherston, *Sixteen Designs for the Theatre* (Oxford University
        Press, 1928).                                                    141
5.24    A satyr in *The Winter's Tale*, Savoy Theatre, 1912. Photograph
        from *The Sketch*, 2 October 1912. Illustrated London News
        Picture Library.                                                 142
5.25    Giovanni da Udine, Festoon in the Loggia of Psyche,
        Farnesina Chigi, Rome.                                           143
6.1     Charles Macklin as Shylock, *c.* 1760.                           145
6.2     Henry Irving as Shylock, 1879. Sketch by J. Bernard Partridge.   147
6.3     Pantalone, from *Compositions de Rhetorique de M. Don Arlequin*
        (Lyons, 1601), a parodic rhetoric. Stanford University Library.  157
6.4     Title page, *The Merchant of Venice*, 1600. Stanford University Library.   161

## Plates

Colour plates are between pages 64 and 65.

  1    Edmund Dulac, illustration for "Full fathom five thy father lies...", *The Tempest*,
       London, 1908. Stanford University Library.
  2    William Hogarth, *Garrick as Richard III*. Reproduced by permission of the Board
       of Trustees of the National Museums and Galleries on Merseyside (Walker Art
       Gallery, Liverpool).

3    Henry Fuseli, Garrick as the Duke of Gloucester in *Richard III*. Kunsthaus Zurich.

4    Johann Zoffany, Garrick and Mrs Pritchard in *Macbeth*. Garrick Club, London.

5    Thomas Rowlandson and A. C. Pugin, Drury Lane Theatre, with *Coriolanus* in progress. From Ackermann's *Microcosm of London*, 1808.

6    Talma in *Hamlet*, color engraving. By permission of the Folger Shakespeare Library.

7    The English Players in the Play Scene from *Hamlet*. Color lithograph. Courtesy of Bibliothèque Nationale de France, Paris.

8    John Singer Sargent, Ellen Terry as Lady Macbeth. Tate Gallery.

9    Henry Wallis (1830–1916), A Sculptor's Workshop, Stratford-Upon-Avon, 1617. From the RSC collection with the permission of the Governors of the Royal Shakespeare Company.

10    The Flower Portrait. Shakespeare Birthplace Trust, Stratford-Upon-Avon.

11    Jim Dine, costume design for Puck, for the Actors' Workshop production of *A Midsummer Night's Dream*, San Francisco, 1966. Watercolor and pencil. The Museum of Modern Art, New York. © 2003 Jim Dine/ Artists Rights Society (ARS), New York. Digital Image © The Museum of Modern Art/ Licensed by Scala/ Art Resource, NY.

12    Jim Dine, costume design for Titania. Watercolor and pencil. The Museum of Modern Art, New York. © 2003 Jim Dine/ Artists Rights Society (ARS), New York. Digital Image © The Museum of Modern Art/ Licensed by Scala/ Art Resource, NY.

13    Quentin Metsys the Younger, Elizabeth I (The Sieve Portrait). Pinacoteca Nazionale, Siena.

14    Giulio Romano, Jove seducing Olimpia. Fresco in the Palazzo Tè, Mantua. Copyright Scala/ Art Resource New York.

15    Giulio Romano, Cupid and Psyche in bed. Fresco in the Palazzo Tè, Mantua. Copyright Scala/ Art Resource New York.

16    Giulio Romano, *Ceres*. Louvre, Paris. Copyright Scala/ Art Resource New York.

# Preface and Acknowledgments

My subject is Shakespeare's history—like all histories, a thing constructed over time, not a set of facts but a complex of interpretations of many different kinds of evidence. The changing construction of what we mean by Shakespeare has determined not only his plays' history on the stage, but their textual history as well, and their vision of history—and I include in this narrative the history that is Shakespeare's changing biography, since it depends heavily on the plays. I focus here particularly on the changing relations of text, performance and interpretation; and my assumption is that these relations are always contingent. I mean by this not merely that our ways of dealing with Shakespeare's text affect the way the plays are performed, but that, more powerfully if less visibly, the history of performance is also the history of the text, and of our interpretation of it, and thereby of what we mean by Shakespeare.

I focus not on the texts but on the history of performance because that is really all there is. Every text we have of Shakespeare, even the very earliest, derives from the stage and has been through some editorial procedure, if only the procedure involved in translating a performing script into a book—a process that in itself is a more complex matter than we are commonly aware. What we have of the Shakespeare text, all we have ever had, is a set of versions with no original. Our editorial assumptions implicitly postulate an original, the manuscript in Shakespeare's hand that we are undertaking to reinvent; but even if such a figment existed, it would not be the stable text we want for this central author in our literary canon. Playhouse scripts were characteristically unstable, designed to be realized on the stage, and designed to change in the process of that realization. The actors started with the playwright's script, but the play took shape as a collaborative effort. My book is about the changing implications, over the centuries, of that collaboration, never an equal partnership, at times amicable, and at other times tense or even hostile.

If the nature of theatrical representation is a central theme throughout the book, part of what makes the topic complex and interesting is that there has been no consensus, over the centuries, about what it is that theater represents. Historically, we may view the transformations of the Shakespearean stage as a debate between performance as presentation—of a script or text, whether modified or not—and performance as representation—of the reality behind the text, the events, whether historical or fictional, that the play purports to bring to life. From the late eighteenth century until well into the twentieth, while Shakespeare's continuing vitality was always acknowledged to reside in his fecund imaginative power and unsurpassed poetry, the validity and authority of the plays were increasingly claimed to lie in their truth to history, a claim which was supported by archeologically accurate costumes and settings. The history in question, however, was not Shakespeare's—theater managers did not, that is, undertake to produce the dramas as the playwright had imagined them and as his audiences would have seen them—but that of his characters, despite the obvious fact that an authentic Henry V is quite a different matter from an authentic Portia or Bottom or Prospero. The development of such assumptions is the subject of my first two chapters. Chapter 3 extends the passion for history into the biographical sphere: the search for an authentic Shakespearean drama was also the search for an authentic Shakespeare. The three final chapters, focusing on three different kinds of historical questions, consider three disparate examples of the intersection of text, interpretation, performance and history, in *A Midsummer Night's Dream*, *The Winter's Tale*, and *The Merchant of Venice*.

This book itself has a short history but a long archeology. It is for the most part based on my Clark Lectures, delivered at Trinity College, Cambridge, in 1996; and it is a pleasure to acknowledge first the most hospitable of hosts and sympathetic of audiences. The earliest version of the first three chapters was written in 1979 for the Baltimore Museum of Art, at the invitation of Jay Fisher, then Associate Curator of Prints, Drawings and Photographs, and delivered in a lecture series related to an exhibition of Théodore Chassériau's illustrations for *Othello*. The series also included talks by Martin Meisel and Michael Fried, dear friends who remain a constant source of inspiration and learning. My lecture was subsequently reworked, and I took it to a number of art museums and universities with the Folger Shakespeare Library's wonderful traveling exhibition *Shakespeare:The Globe and theWorld* in 1980 and 1981; though for that and subsequent versions Chassériau, whom I had never been able to work up much enthusiasm for, was omitted. The talk remained, in various incarnations, a staple of my lecture repertory. It was a pleasure finally to revise and expand it into a more detailed treatment for the Clark Lectures, and now, with its publication, to put it to rest. Chapter 6, on Shylock, was not part of the Clark Lectures, but is based on a plenary talk delivered at the International Shakespeare Association meeting in Valencia, Spain, in 2001. A version of it appears under the title "Shylock's Tribe" in *Shakespeare and the Mediterranean: The Selected Proceedings of the International Shakespeare Association World Congress, Valencia, 2001*, edited by Tom Clayton, Susan Brock, and Vicente Forés (Newark: University of Delaware Press; London: Associated University Presses, 2003). A version of Chapter 3 appears under the title "Original Copies" in *Word and Image* 19.1 (2003), and I am indebted to the editor, Adrian Randolph, for advice, information, and a good deal of material assistance with the illustrations.

I am especially indebted, as is anyone who works in this field, to a number of classics of theater history, of which I single out only a few that have served as my constant guides: George C. D. O'Dell's *Shakespeare from Betterton to Irving*, W. Moelwyn Merchant's *Shakespeare and the Artist*, and Martin Meisel's *Realizations*. In addition, three recent works have proved especially enlightening: Dennis Kennedy's *Looking at Shakespeare*, the collaborative volume *Shakespeare: An Illustrated Stage History*, edited by Jonathan Bate and Russell Jackson, and my superb student Richard Schoch's *Shakespeare's Victorian Stage*. Over the years I have learned much about my subject from both the work and the friendship of Anne Barton and John Barton, and of John Stokes, Michael Dobson, Peter Holland, David Kastan, Lois Potter, and A. R. Braunmuller. Stanford's Rare Books Librarian John Mustain has proved expert, indefatigable and miraculously good-natured on my behalf. I am also happy to acknowledge the invariably responsive and helpful staff of the Folger Shakespeare Library, and seventeen years of splendid graduate students at Stanford, of whom I single out, for the light they shed specifically on the present project, Richard Schoch, Anston Bosman, James Marino, and Richard Preiss. Stanford's institutional support has been generous and unfailing, and a Guggenheim Fellowship gave me the time to convert four elaborate slide lectures into a lavishly illustrated book. The suggestions, editorial acumen, and friendship of Josie Dixon, at Palgrave Macmillan, made the whole project both possible and pleasant. Paula Kennedy and Emily Rosser have been the most patient and helpful of editors, and deserve much of the credit for negotiating the minefields of picture permissions. Finally, the dedication acknowledges one who has been, over the years, the best of readers and dearest of friends.

Every effort has been made to trace all copyright holders, but if any have been inadvertently overlooked, the publisher will be pleased to make the necessary arrangements at the first opportunity.

# ONE

## Imagining Shakespeare

I have described Shakespeare's drama, in its essence and throughout its history, as collaborative. The collaboration was between author and actor, script or text and performance or realization; and it was, for the most part, not an equal partnership. In most cases in Shakespeare's time, the playwright was not at all at the center of this collaboration; he was an employee of the company, and once he delivered the script his interest in it, and his authority over it, was ended. Shakespeare is one of a small number of exceptions, in that he was both a shareholder and principal actor in the company he wrote for, and thus was literally his own boss; but all this means is that he would have been involved in more parts of the collaboration than other playwrights were.

I begin, then, with an absolutely basic question about our sense of Shakespearean drama: when we read the text of a play, what do we assume that text represents—what do we *see*? The simplest answer is that we see only words on a page; and there is the first problem: unlike most other major playwrights that we read—Ben Jonson, Congreve, Shaw—Shakespeare never conceived, or even re-conceived, his plays as texts to be read. They were scripts, not books; the only readers were the performers, and the function of the script was to be realized on the stage. For Shakespeare, there always was an imagination intervening between his text and its audience, the imagination of actor, director, producer—roles that, in his own time, Shakespeare played himself. The one role he apparently did not play was that of textual editor, the crucial role when the script became a book—when, for whatever reason, it became expedient to publish it.

The characteristic instability of playhouse scripts can be seen in the variety of Shakespeare texts that has come down to us. There are, for example, three versions of *Hamlet*, two of *Othello* and *Lear*; and, indeed, all the plays that have survived in both quarto and folio versions show significant differences between the two. There is clear evidence within individual texts of revisions: there seems to have been an early version of *Twelfth Night* without Feste, the two quartos and the folio texts of *Romeo and Juliet* have three quite different versions of Juliet's balcony soliloquy, the play's most famous speech, *Love's Labour's Lost* includes an extended passage in two different versions, *Macbeth* includes a demonstrably non-Shakespearean scene, and so forth. Such things suggest that for each revival the text was reconsidered and revised; and (as the *Macbeth* example indicates) not necessarily by Shakespeare. For Shakespeare and his colleagues the text of a play was simply the basis for an individual season's production, not a finished product but the first stage of a collaborative process. And this also means that the texts that have come down to us, preserved in the various quartos and more formally in the first folio, published seven years after Shakespeare's death, constitute essentially a collection of versions of any particular play. Historically speaking, what our text of *Hamlet* or *Lear* represents is an anthology of productions.

This is, for us, a fairly special notion of drama. We can see how special it is by comparing it with the attitude of Shakespeare's friend and colleague Ben Jonson toward the texts of his plays. Unlike Shakespeare, Jonson took a good deal of trouble over their publication. And the texts that he published were, he tells us, significantly different from the texts audiences heard in the playhouse. For example, Jonson's tragedy *Sejanus* was originally written in collaboration with another playwright; that was the version the actors performed. But for the printed text, Jonson removed his collaborator's scenes and replaced them with ones of his own. He also added a good deal of historical material: the play in print was to be both an authentic representation of the events depicted in it, and authentically his own. He is lavish in praise of his collaborator; but he also pointedly omits any mention of his name, and since there are no other records, we can now only guess who he may have been. Jonson, in effect, succeeded in suppressing the production, and replaced it with an independent text, which he consistently refers to, moreover, not as a play but as a poem. In such a form, the drama of *Sejanus* no longer requires the mediation of an acting company for its realization. The play is now a transaction between the author and the individual reader, and the only performance takes place in the reader's imagination. Several of Jonson's contemporaries—John Webster, for example—went a step further, and implied, with varying degrees of resentment, that the actors had misrepresented their texts, either by cutting or by revision. Jonson himself blames both the actors and the audience for the failure of his comedy *The New Inn*, declaring on the title page that "it was never acted, but most negligently played by some, the King's servants, and more squeamishly beheld and censured by others, the King's subjects." For these playwrights the text is something different from, independent of, and only inadequately represented by the production.

The publisher Humphrey Moseley's introductory epistle to the 1647 Beaumont and Fletcher folio explains the matter:

> When these *Comedies* and *Tragedies* were presented on the Stage, the *Actours* omitted some *Scenes* and Passages (with the *Authour's* consent) as occasion led them.... But now you have both All that was *Acted*, and all that was not; even the perfect full Originalls without the least mutilation; So that were the *Authours* living...they themselves would challenge neither more nor lesse then what is here published.

The printed text, in Mosely's account, includes both authors' and players' versions—"all that was acted and all that was not"—and implies that the cuts were both authorized and determined by the occasion: the actors omitted scenes and speeches to fit the play into the normal performing time of two hours, and otherwise varied the script according to their sense of the audience. The play might change, then, from season to season, from playhouse to playhouse, even, if occasion required, from performance to performance—the play before the king was not the same as the play at the Globe, and neither of them was the text that came from the author's pen, which these publishers assert is the true play, "the perfect full originals without the least mutilation." What the performance does in this account is mutilate the perfect original.

But if for the actors the text was not the play, what was the relationship between the two? What kind of authority did Shakespeare's, Jonson's or Webster's manuscripts have, and what kind of responsibility did playhouse practice feel toward them? Shakespeare seems, in *Hamlet*, to be especially concerned about the dangers of improvisation:

> let those that play your clowns speak no more than is set down for them. For there be of them that will themselves laugh, to set on some quantity of barren spectators to laugh too, though in the meantime some necessary question of the play be then to be considered. (3.2.42ff.)

One could press very hard on that "necessary question of the play"—necessary for whom? Are the author's interests the same as the actor's? In Hamlet's first scene with the ghost, Hamlet's own behavior, the jokes about the voice in the "cellerage" and all the rushing about the stage to avoid the "old mole" beneath will look to an audience without access to the script like a particularly disruptive kind of comic improvisation. This is Shakespeare making the anti-textual textual, but it also puts Shakespeare the actor in league with the audience against Shakespeare the playwright, and it strikingly reveals a divided loyalty.

I am concerned precisely with that tension between text and performance; for as editors, critics, and even as readers, we have always shared, in profound and unexamined ways, that original divided loyalty. Our scholarly texts, for all their line numbers, collations, glosses, commentaries, are no more stable than the playhouse script: every edition of Shakespeare is different from every other one—these are performances too, eliciting from the obscurities and confusions of the original texts any number of different but equally coherent readings. There is, of course, very little evidence that will reveal to us the nature of a performing text in Shakespeare's theater; but there is a little. There are those notorious "bad" quartos that seem to derive directly from performing texts, or even conceivably (like the first quarto of *Hamlet*) from a recollection of performance itself, and whose evidence, therefore, in this respect, is not bad, but excellent. If we were less concerned with the authority of texts and more concerned with the nature of plays, these would be the good quartos.

Some direct evidence survives in three pre-Restoration promptbooks, of *Macbeth, Measure for Measure* and the two parts of *Henry the Fourth*.[1] The first two are marked-up texts from a folio now in the library of the University of Padua, the third is a scribal transcription based on the quartos. I have written in some detail about these; here I simply describe them and offer some brief examples. The *Henry the Fourth*, which dates from the early 1620s, was prepared for a private production at a country estate. It underwent far more radical revision than the other two, amalgamating the two plays and reducing their approximately 6000 lines to roughly 3500, but also including a substantial amount of additional original material. This manuscript reveals a great deal about both the sophistication of amateur theater and the way a popular Shakespearean text was regarded in the early seventeenth century; and the proprietary attitude of the reviser toward the text is especially noteworthy. But it also, as a private enterprise, represents a special case, and is therefore less useful for my purposes than the other two. These have been dated between 1625 and 1635, and were apparently prepared by a professional hand for a professional company.[2] About their actual use we can say nothing, but they allow us to see what a performing text of Shakespeare looked like within a decade or two of the playwright's death.

The Padua *Macbeth* has small and apparently arbitrary cuts in the first act. Moments in the text that have troubled later editors, such as the notorious muddle of the Captain's account of the decisive battle in which Macbeth distinguished himself, are left intact; indeed, there is only a single, minor cut before Act 1, scene 7. But here is Macbeth's first soliloquy as it appears in the promptbook:

> If it were done when 'tis done, then 'twere well
> It were done quickly. If th'assassination
> Could trammel up the consequence, and catch
> With his surcease, success; that but this blow
> Might be the be all, and the end all.
> He's here in double trust;
> First, as I am his kinsman and his subject,
> Strong both against the deed. Then, as his host,
> Who should against his murderer shut the door,
> Not bear the knife myself. Besides this Duncan
> Hath borne his faculties so meek, hath been
> So clear in his great office, that his virtues
> Will plead like angels, trumpet-tongued, against
> The deep damnation of his taking-off;
> And pity, like a naked newborn babe,
> Striding the blast, or heaven's cherubin, horsed
> Upon the sightless couriers of the air,
> Shall blow the horrid deed in every eye,
> That tears shall drown the wind.
> How now, what news?

That is, no bank and school of time, no bloody instructions, no poisoned chalice, no spur to prick the sides of my intent, no vaulting ambition that o'erleaps itself and falls.

Wholesale cutting begins in Act 2. All of the Porter's speech goes (as it often has done ever since); with it go most of the exchange between Macbeth and the murderers, the whole of 3.6 between Lenox and the Lord, most of Malcolm's interview with Macduff, in which Malcolm tests Macduff by claiming to practice monstrous vices. In all, 292 of the play's 2084 lines are cut, almost 15 percent of this shortest of Shakespeare's tragedies. I pause over what is perhaps, for us, the most striking of the deletions. Macbeth's reaction to the death of Lady Macbeth in the Padua text reads this way:

> She should have died hereafter;
> There would have been a time for such a word.
> Tomorrow and tomorrow and tomorrow
> Creeps in this petty pace from day to day,
> To the last syllable of recorded time;
> And all our yesterdays have lighted fools
> The way to dusty death. Out, out brief candle,
> Life's but a walking shadow.
> It is a tale
> Told by an idiot, full of sound and fury,
> Signifying nothing.    (5.5.17–28)

What is for us the most striking—and, for our sense of Shakespeare, the most revealing—part of the speech, the self-reflexive poor player who struts and frets his hour upon the stage and then is heard no more, is jettisoned.

The cutting of the Padua folio's *Measure for Measure* seems far more systematic. Long speeches are shortened, debates are tightened and simplified, and—especially—poetic complexity is removed. A certain quality of continuous explanation in the play (a quality that most modern readers would call essential) disappears too: gone are the Duke's opening speech ("Of government the properties to unfold..."), the first fifteen lines of his charge to Angelo ("There is a kind of character in thy life/ That to th'observer doth thy history/ Fully unfold," etc.), and, more strikingly, Claudio's exculpatory account of why he and Juliet never formalized their marriage:

> This came we not to
> Only for propagation of a dower
> Remaining in the coffer of her friends,
> From whom we thought it meet to hide our love
> Till time had made them for us. (1.2.153–7)

Indeed, even Claudio's revelation of Juliet's pregnancy was originally cut—

> But it chances
> The stealth of our most mutual entertainment
> With character too gross is writ on Juliet, (157–9)

but this was subsequently restored with a marginal "stet."

Much of the Duke's explanation to the Friar of why he left his throne has gone—this works unquestionably to the benefit of his logic, if not to the complexity of his character. In Isabella's first interview with Angelo, the arguments on both sides are effectively eviscerated; Figure 1.1 gives a sense of how radical the cutting is (the bracketed sections are to be deleted). Indeed, the omission from this version of what were to become the most famous passages in the play is notable. The only major scene that is left even relatively intact is Isabella's interview with her brother in prison. In all, the reviser cut almost 600 of the play's 2660 lines, or about 22 percent—a larger proportion than the *Macbeth* cuts, but still leaving a longer play.

The cuts in both these texts are for the most part designed simply to shorten the major roles, not, apparently, to adapt the play to any special circumstances—there is no attempt to reduce the number of characters or to alter things that, in later revisions, were felt to be indecorous. The folio texts of both plays, it should be noted, derive from performing texts, *Measure for Measure* apparently from a transcript of the promptbook and *Macbeth* even more directly from a revised and cut script; but within a decade of the volume's publica-

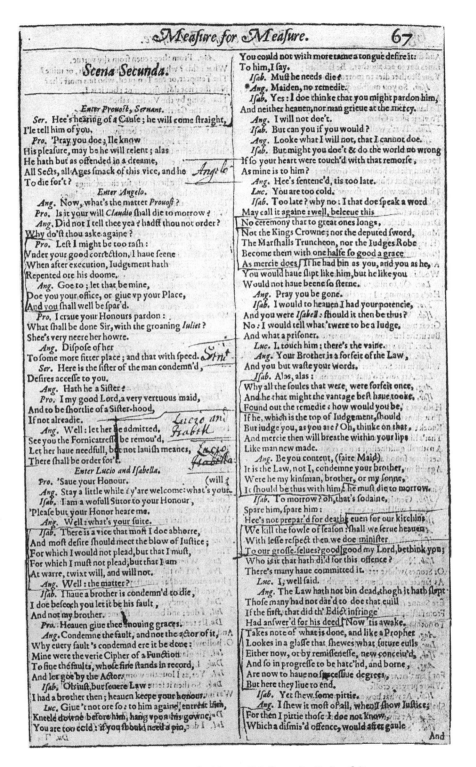

## Scena Secunda.

*Enter Prouoft, Seruant.*

*Ser.* Hee's hearing of a Caufe ; he will come ftraight,
I'le tell him of you.
*Pro.* 'Pray you doe, Ile know
His pleafure, may be he will relent ; alas
He hath but as offended in a dreame,
All Sects, all Ages fmack of this vice, and he
To die for't ?

*Enter Angelo.*

*Ang.* Now, what's the matter *Prouoft* ?
*Pro.* Is it your will *Claudio* fhall die to morrow ?
*Ang.* Did not I tell thee yea ? hadft thou not order ?
Why do'ft thou aske againe ?
*Pro.* Left I might be too rafh :
Vnder your good correction, I haue feene
When after execution, Iudgement hath
Repented ore his doome.
*Ang.* Goe to ; let that be mine,
Doe you your office, or giue vp your Place,
And you fhall well be fpar'd.
*Pro.* I craue your Honours pardon :
What fhall be done Sir, with the groaning *Iuliet* ?
Shee's very neere her howre.
*Ang.* Difpofe of her
To fome more fitter place ; and that with fpeed.
*Ser.* Here is the fifter of the man condemn'd,
Defires accefse to you.
*Ang.* Hath he a Sifter ?
*Pro.* I my good Lord, a very vertuous maid,
And to be fhortlie of a Sifter-hood,
If not alreadie.
*Ang.* Well : let her be admitted,
See you the Fornicatrefse be remou'd,
Let her haue needfull, but not lauifh meanes,
There fhall be order for't.

*Enter Lucio and Ifabella.*

*Pro.* 'Saue your Honour. (will ?
*Ang.* Stay a little while : ty'are welcome: what's your
*Ifab.* I am a wofull Sutor to your Honour,
'Pleafe but your Honor heare me.
*Ang.* Well : what's your fuite.
*Ifab.* There is a vice that moft I doe abhorre,
And moft defire fhould meet the blow of Iuftice ;
For which I would not plead, but that I muft,
For which I muft not plead, but that I am
At warre, twixt will, and will not.
*Ang.* Well : the matter ?
*Ifab.* I haue a brother is condemn'd to die,
I doe befeech you let it be his fault,
And not my brother.
*Pro.* Heauen giue thee mouing graces.
*Ang.* Condemne the fault, and not the actor of it,
Why euery fault 's condemn'd ere it be done :
Mine were the verie Cipher of a Function
To fine the faults, whofe fine ftands in record,
And let goe by the Actors.
*Ifab.* Oh iuft, but feuere Law :
I had a brother then ; heauen keepe your honour,
*Luc.* Giue 't not ore fo : to him againe, entreat him,
Kneele downe before him, hang vpon his gowne,
You are too cold : if you fhould need a pin,

You could not with more tame a tongue defire it:
To him, I fay.
*Ifab.* Muft he needs die ?
*Ang.* Maiden, no remedie.
*Ifab.* Yes : I doe thinke that you might pardon him,
And neither heauen, nor man grieue at the mercy.
*Ang.* I will not doe't.
*Ifab.* But can you if you would ?
*Ang.* Looke what I will not, that I cannot doe.
*Ifab.* But might you doe't & do the world no wrong
If fo your heart were touch'd with that remorfe,
As mine is to him ?
*Ang.* Hee's fentenc'd, tis too late.
*Luc.* You are too cold.
*Ifab.* Too late ? why no : I that doe fpeak a word
May call it againe : well, beleeue this
No ceremony that to great ones longs,
Not the Kings Crowne ; nor the deputed fword,
The Marfhalls Truncheon, nor the Iudges Robe
Become them with one halfe fo good a grace
As mercie does. If he had bin as you, and you as he,
You would haue flipt like him, but he like you
Would not haue beene fo fterne.
*Ang.* Pray you be gone.
*Ifab.* I would to heauen I had your potencie,
And you were *Ifabell* : fhould it then be thus ?
No : I would tell what'twere to be a Iudge,
And what a prifoner.
*Luc.* I, touch him ; there's the vaine.
*Ang.* Your Brother is a forfeit of the Law,
And you but wafte your words.
*Ifab.* Alas, alas :
Why all the foules that were, were forfeit once,
And he that might the vantage beft haue tooke,
Found out the remedie : how would you be,
If he, which is the top of Iudgement, fhould
But iudge you, as you are ? Oh, thinke on that,
And mercie then will breathe within your lips
Like man new made.
*Ang.* Be you content, (faire Maid)
It is the Law, not I, condemne your brother,
Were he my kinfman, brother, or my fonne,
It fhould be thus with him : he muft die to morrow.
*Ifab.* To morrow ? oh, that's fodaine,
Spare him, fpare him :
Hee's not prepar'd for death, euen for our kitchins
We kill the fowle of feafon : fhall we ferue heauen
With lefse refpect then we doe minifter
To our groffe-felues ? good, good my Lord, bethink you ;
Who is it that hath di'd for this offence ?
There's many haue committed it.
*Luc.* I, well faid.
*Ang.* The Law hath not bin dead, thogh it hath flept
Thofe many had not dar'd to doe that euill
If the firft, that did th' Edict infringe
Had anfwer'd for his deed. Now 'tis awake,
Takes note of what is done, and like a Prophet
Lookes in a glaffe that fhewes what future euills
Either now, or by remifseneffe, new conceiu'd,
And fo in progreffe to be hatch'd, and borne,
Are now to haue no fucceffiue degrees,
But here they liue to end.
*Ifab.* Yet fhew fome pittie.
*Ang.* I fhew it moft of all, when I fhow Iuftice ;
For then I pittie thofe I doe not know,
Which a difmis'd offence, would after gaule,

And

tion the King's Men's acting versions were already, for this director, too long and complicated. For modern readers, however, the most striking aspect of the Padua revisions is their systematic deletion of so much that, for almost three centuries, has made Shakespeare distinctive, remarkable, even recognizable—their deletion, in a word, of what we call "Shakespeare": the complex poetry, the rhetorical grandeur; and in fact, in large measure, the bits that became famous. For this reviser, the essential Shakespeare play is action, not poetry. The folio text is, moreover, only where the play starts, not the text to be realized in performance—the Shakespearean text here has no particular integrity, any more than, for the King's Men, Jonson's script of *The New Inn* or Shakespeare's own scripts had had. Obviously the concept of *Macbeth, Measure for Measure, Henry IV*, included broad areas of possibility and difference, and was not at all limited to what was to be found in "the true original copies."

   All this suggests that the text of a play was thought of as distinctly, essentially, by nature, unfixed; always open to revision. This idea makes us very uncomfortable, and even critics who are willing to acknowledge the necessary instability of playhouse scripts in the Renaissance, would probably want to argue that, at least after Shakespeare's death, the "real" Shakespeare play was always what is preserved in the printed text, because all productions ultimately exist in reference to that. This makes perfectly good sense, but it seems to me that it makes sense only because of certain anachronistic assumptions we have about texts: first, that the text is the play, and second, that texts themselves are essentially fixed, and represent the final form of the work, the form that embodies the author's intentions. This assumes, in turn, a modern norm: that Shakespeare revised until he was finished, and then the play was published. But if publication was not the end in view, as is clearly the case, why would any version be considered final? The claim of finality might be arguable in the case of a playwright like Jonson, who did revise his plays for publication and oversaw their printing; but in such instances the text clearly is *not* the play. The text is a book; the play has been left behind, disowned, even suppressed.

Behind Shakespeare's view of the relation between texts and productions and the antithetical view of Jonson, or Webster, or the publisher of Beaumont and Fletcher, lies a much more basic question: what do we think a play is? What is essential to it or real about it? Is the text the real thing, and is any production merely a *version* of the play, occasional and ephemeral? Or is the text merely the basis of the play, not the play itself, which must be realized—made real—in production? Or is the text only what remains, the best the playwright (or in the case of about half Shakespeare's plays, his executors) can do to preserve some vestige of the real play, which is the experience of the audience in the theater?

Suppose we press further and ask what is real or essential about the text. The words? They create the play. But the words are spoken by characters, and in production require actors to express them, and it certainly looks as if the dialogue is a function of the characters, not the other way round. This is, of course, an illusion—the characters are the lines they speak—but it is, in a sense, the illusion that is at the heart of drama, what drama is all about: without this illusion, there is no play. Aristotle, however, said that neither the language nor the characters were essential to drama, but the action was: do we believe this? Is the action not determined precisely by the characters and the lines they speak? What about a tradition like the *commedia dell'arte*, in which a potentially infinite number of actions is performed by a limited and invariable cast of characters—in which, that is, the characters are essential, but the action is unscripted and infinitely mutable, changing not only from play to play but even from performance to performance? Indeed, we might argue that this is the real essence of theater: not the texts of plays at all, but the performance of actors.

My point is not to settle the matter, but to indicate that we have had, historically, a number of very different ways of conceiving of drama, and most of them are mutually exclusive. There is nothing anomalous in this: theater is the most complex of arts, and its very complexity implies, and indeed demands, contradictory responses. I turn now to some examples of how those complex and contradictory assumptions have conditioned our sense of theater from Shakespeare's time forward, and have thereby conditioned our sense of Shakespeare. These are documents in the history of our theatrical imagination.

I begin with the idea of theater itself, and with some examples roughly contemporaneous with Shakespeare. A play can be imagined as a particular performance taking place on a particular stage. Figure 1.2 shows the performance of *Oedipus* on the opening night of the Teatro Olimpico in Vicenza in 1585, as depicted in a fresco in the lobby. The theater was designed by Andrea Palladio for the Olympic Academy, a group of Vicentine citizens devoted to the study and performance of classical drama. The fresco is intended not as an illustration to the play but as a memorial to the opening of the first great neoclassic theater in Italy. The most impressive element in the painting by far is the architecture, which dwarfs both actors and spectators. Nevertheless, this fresco is among the most detailed and informative visual records of attitudes toward both ancient drama and stage practice surviving from the period. Though the performers wear classical robes, the priests surrounding Oedipus are identifiable as priests because of their quite contemporary bishops' miters. The main actors are bare faced, but the pages in attendance carry masks. The relation between authenticity and anachronism is a critical one here, and this is an example I shall return to. It is significant that the Italian translation commissioned for the production was

*Figure 1.2*   The performance of *Edipo Tiranno* (*Oedipus Rex*) at the opening of the Teatro Olimpico in Vicenza, 1585.

published for the occasion, but without illustrations: the record of perform-ance was a function of the theater, not of the book.

Figure 1.3 shows a quite different sort of image, again conditioned by attitudes toward classical drama, and in which the theater is again more important than the play. This is the closest thing we have to an eyewitness drawing of an Elizabethan public theater, an early copy of the Dutch traveler Johannes de Witt's sketch of the Swan playhouse in London around 1595. De Witt was particularly interested in this theater because it seemed to him to preserve the form of ancient Roman theaters, and he believed therefore that a classical dramatic tradition had survived in England. The sketch originally formed part of a letter to a friend in Holland, who transcribed it into his journal—it is the journal that has survived. A scene is in progress, but de Witt's commentary makes no reference to the play; for his purposes, presumably any play will do, but given his interests, it is probably significant that the play is modern, not classical—this is not a piece of historical reconstruction, but shows what was actually being performed. The essential element for de Witt is the fact that the theater can be described with the terminology of Roman amphitheaters—*orchestra, sedelia, planities sive arena, proscaenium, mimorum aedes*.

De Witt's Swan is a theater with actors, but with only the merest gesture toward an audience, and not, moreover, where one would expect them, in

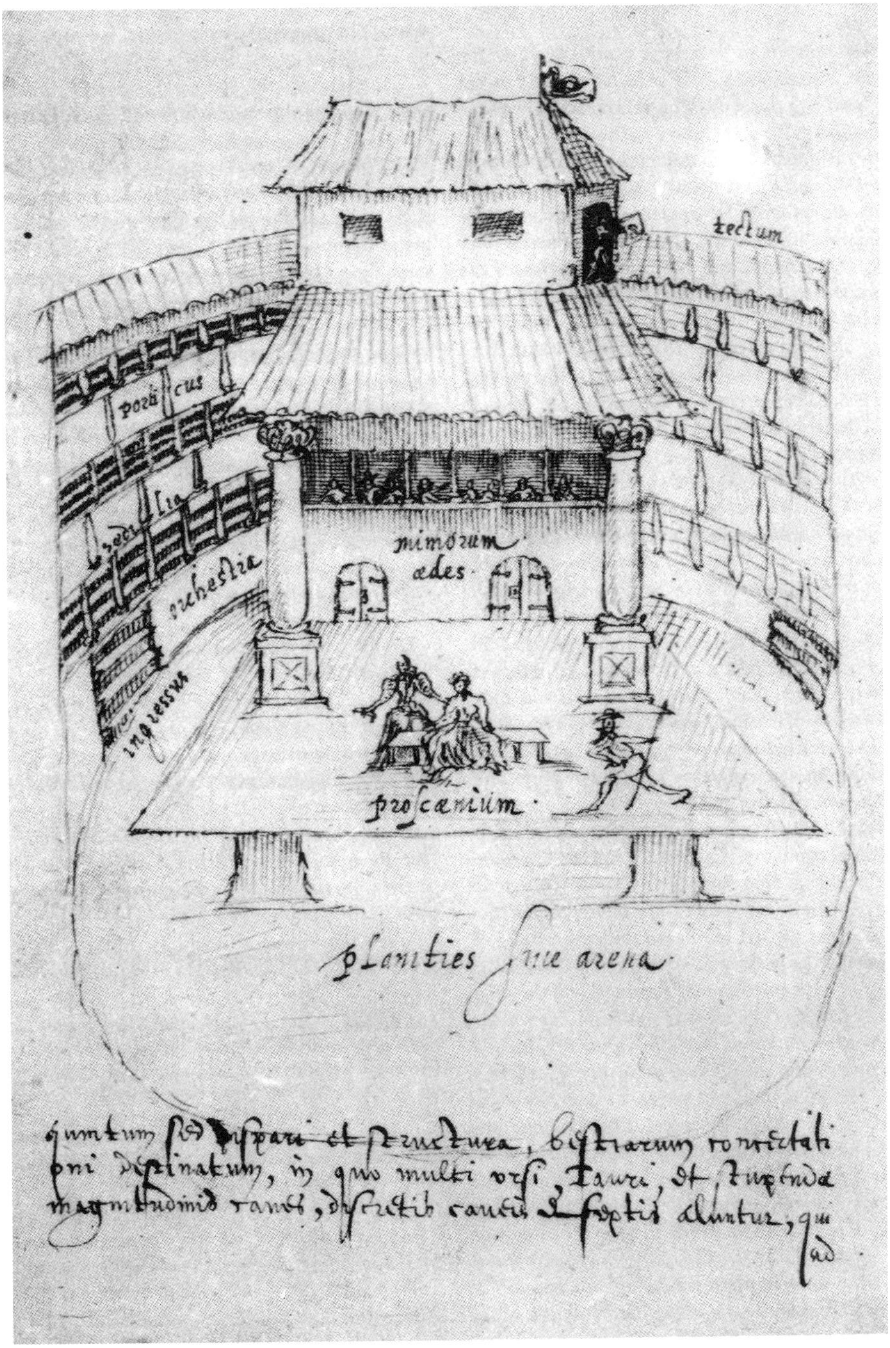

Figure 1.3    Arend van Buchel after Johannes de Witt,
the Swan Playhouse, London, c. 1595.

the *orchestra* or *sedelia*, but in the gallery above the stage. This element of the drawing has occasioned much learned debate. The stage gallery was a playing area, though we know that seats were also sold there from time to time. So finding spectators in the gallery is not in itself problematic; the problem is that there are no spectators anywhere else. Was de Witt perhaps recording a rehearsal, when the public was not admitted? But the flag above the stage is flying: flags were raised above Elizabethan playhouses only when performances were in progress. Are we, then, perhaps trying to read the drawing too literally? Should we imagine an audience in the *sedelia*? The sketch is, after all, an amateur copy of an amateur drawing, which is undertaking not to provide a record of the Elizabethan stage in action but to show its relation to the classical stage of Vitruvius; and it does this somewhat schematically. Still, the exclusion of the audience from a theater with a play in progress is surely not inconsequential, if we are considering the idea of a theater.

Illustrations designed to accompany the texts of plays provide an opposite kind of example, in which the exclusion of the audience is the essence of the play's transformation into a book. Figure 1.4 is a woodcut used in the third quarto of the anonymous tragedy *Arden of Feversham*, a relatively late edition published in 1633—the two previous quartos, of 1592 and 1599, had not been illustrated. This image illustrates a reading text of the play, at a time when it was probably no longer in the theatrical repertory. It depicts the murder scene, not entirely accurately (the second woman, on the left, is not present during the murder, and in the play all three murderers stab Arden with a single knife), but if it is intended to represent the scene as if performed—to depict, that is, not simply the action, but the action as taking

Figure 1.4    *Arden of Feversham* (1633), woodcut illustration on the verso of the title page.

place on a stage—we must imagine the stage. There is no sense of an audience or a theater, least of all the sort of public theater where such a play would have been performed—the Swan, the Rose, the Globe—with its architectural façade and minimal settings. (There is in fact no record of any performance of *Arden*, though it has all the earmarks of a popular play.) The drama represented here consists only of its action, and if we did not know this was an illustration of a play, we would not identify the setting as a stage. The same woodcut was used for a broadside ballad about the murder printed in the same year, to which it was obviously felt to be equally appropriate.

The title page illustration to the 1615 quarto of Thomas Kyd's *Spanish Tragedy*, in Figure 1.5, takes a little more into account: it acknowledges that dialogue is an essential component of the action of a play. Unlike the *Arden* woodcut, however, this is not in any sense a scene from this tremendously popular play, which was still very much in the repertory. It is rather a summary of the central action, conflating two separate moments. In the drama, Hieronymo is alone when he discovers his son's body; the murder of Horatio, his lover Bel-Imperia's cries for help, and her sequestration by the villains Lorenzo and Balthazar, all take place before he enters. Moreover, the dialogue that comes in ribbons from the characters' mouths exists nowhere in the text; it

Figure 1.5    Thomas Kyd, *The Spanish Tragedy* (1615), woodcut from the title page.

has been invented for the picture. Despite the fact that this illustrates a printed version of the play, the action here departs radically from its script—the scene depicted has been improvised by the artist, as if the play were not a text but a scenario. The sources of this kind of representation are images that, however dramatic, have no connection with plays or theater—early Annunciation scenes, for example, in which "Ave gratia plena" emanates from the angelic messenger's mouth. And once again, though we would certainly, because of the context, be aware of the setting as a stage, there is nothing suggesting a theater or an audience.

Figure 1.6 has become famous as the earliest representation of a Shakespearean subject: it purports to be a scene from *Titus Andronicus*. The name of the emblem writer Henry Peacham appears on the same page, with an obscure date that has been read as 1594 or 1595; it is not clear, however, that these have anything to do with the drawing. The dubiousness of the sketch's provenance extends to its subject matter as well: Queen Tamora pleads with Titus for the life of her two sons, who kneel on the right, guarded by Aaron the Moor, as two soldiers watch. These are all characters in the play, and they are certainly performing a scene; but just as in the *Spanish Tragedy* illustration, the scene is not in the play—or at least, not in its text. There is a portion of the opening scene that includes all the figures depicted in the drawing, but at this point Aaron is a prisoner along with the two sons, and could not be standing over them with drawn sword. Recently the scholar

Figure 1.6    Henry Peacham (?), c. 1595, a scene from *Titus Andronicus*.
Longleat Portland Papers I f. 159v.

June Schlueter has undertaken to link the drawing not to Shakespeare's play but to its putative source, the lost play *Titus and Vespasian*, which appears to survive in a German version of the play as it was performed by English actors traveling on the continent.[3] The drawing is by no means a precise match for the scene Schlueter cites in *Titus and Vespasian* (and if she is correct, the central figure is the emperor, not Titus), but it is arguably closer than it is to any scene in *Titus Andronicus*.

Below the drawing is a dramatic extract. It is this that identifies the drawing as relating to Shakespeare's *Titus*, but the passage transcribed is not simply a quotation from the play. It combines passages from two separate scenes: an exchange between Tamora and Titus from Act 1 is answered by a speech of Aaron's from Act 5—apparently the writer of the text, not finding a scene in the play that accorded with the drawing, decided to invent one. It has generally been assumed, reasonably, that the scribe and the artist are therefore not the same person, though several recent commentators have observed that the careful arrangement of the page argues against artist and scribe working separately and at different times, and that therefore both the scene and the text more likely represent a conspectus or symbolic summary of the action. In either case, the text here is fully dependent on the performance, and the scribe has no more compunction about revising Shakespeare's text to fit the representation than the artist of the *Spanish Tragedy* illustration had, or than the promptbook editors of *Macbeth* and *Measure for Measure* and the actors of Jonson's *New Inn* were to have thirty years later.

I turn now to a group of examples that make a quite antithetical assumption, that make theater inhere not in the particular—occasions, playhouses, plays, characters—but in the general. Sebastiano Serlio's generic stage sets constitute perhaps the most famous and influential idea of theater in the Renaissance. Figure 1.7 is the Tragic Scene. In 1545 Serlio, as part of a corpus of architecture, devised prototype stage sets for the three classic kinds of drama, the tragic, the comic, and the satiric or pastoral. These are models to be employed in the theater of a noble house in the neoclassic style. Serlio is adapting Vitruvius to the uses of the Italian Renaissance; Vitruvius has a chapter on public theaters, but Serlio assumes that any great house will include a theater of its own. The tragic setting consists of palaces and temples, aristocratic and public buildings, and monuments. Its perspective is open, with a triumphal arch at its apex, and beyond the arch a forum of architectural hieroglyphs—pyramid, obelisk; the mysterious embodiments of ancient wisdom.

Figure 1.8, the comic setting, in contrast, consists of middle-class architecture: Serlio says these are merchants' houses; they belong to a Renaissance Italian cityscape. A shop is visible halfway back on the left, and the perspective is closed by the façade of a Renaissance church with its medieval tower,

*Figure 1.7*    Sebastiano Serlio, The Tragic Scene, from *Architettura*, 1545.

partly decayed, the only visible link with a monumental past, and an index as well to the passage of time. In the right foreground Serlio has placed a brothel, inscribed with the name Rufia, presumably the madam. No such character figures in any play of Plautus or Terence; Rufia is in fact not a proper name at all, but the Italian comedy's generic term for a prostitute or madam—Florio, using the form *roffiana*, translates it "a woman bawd"; the word is cognate with *ruffian*. Serlio's comedy is modern.

The satiric or pastoral setting, in Figure 1.9, consists of rustic buildings, trees, and a mass of birds filling what is visible of the sky. Its architecture consists of utilitarian huts; the man-made is visibly overwhelmed by the surrounding nature. This setting makes no temporal assumptions at all: it is a world that has always been with us. But its action also takes place somewhere altogether different—in the woods, in nature, without the order imposed by architectural façades, and barely controlled by symmetry. For Serlio, then, the tragic is urban, noble, ancient, open, and mysterious; the comic urban, middle-class, modern, closed and rational; the pastoral rustic, humble,

*Figure 1.8*   Sebastiano Serlio, The Comic Scene, from *Architettura*, 1545.

timeless, and natural or wild. The kinds of drama are internally consistent and mutually exclusive, both topographically and chronologically.

As summaries of a Renaissance idea of theater, these rigid and consistent realizations are clearly much more relevant to Italian drama of the period than to most of what was presented on English stages, though even this generalization, as we shall see, requires some serious qualification. But the Serlian models appear in English sources too, and were, indeed, influential throughout Europe. How do they relate to the obvious fluidity of Renaissance drama, to the mobility of its action (which contemporary classicists like Sidney complained of) and especially to its fondness for, and even reliance on, anachronism? The Peacham sketch in Figure 1.6 is in obvious ways much truer to Shakespearean conceptions of theater than Serlio's generic settings are. Consider the costumes. Titus (or Vespasian, as the case may be) is in

*Figure 1.9*   Sebastiano Serlio, The Satiric or Pastoral Scene, from *Architettura*, 1545.

Roman dress, and Tamora is in some sort of generalized royal dress, vaguely medieval—certainly neither Elizabethan nor Roman. The sons and Aaron are in ambiguous costumes; the sleeves are Elizabethan, and what they wear around their middles could be either Elizabethan pants or Roman military skirts, though the sash on the son on the left is the same as Titus's, and is presumably intended as Roman. But the guards are fully outfitted Elizabethan soldiers. This all looks inept and unconvincing to us, but the inconsistency and anachronism are clearly essential elements, and not included casually or thoughtlessly—this is a point to which I shall return. Elizabethan drama is characteristically inconsistent in just this way, its reality infinitely adjustable. The costumes in the sketch are designed to indicate the characters' roles and their relation to each other, and most important, their relation to us. A few elements are included to suggest the classical setting, but there is no attempt to mirror a world or re-create a historical moment. And, as we saw in Figure 1.2, despite the Olympic Academy's commitment to history and archeology, the *Oedipus* fresco in Vicenza reveals a concept of tragedy that is similarly inconsistent, utilizing explicitly anachronistic details to establish its reality: Oedipus's costume is vaguely classical, but the priests wear bishops' miters and copes. The figures are thereby accounted for, located in relation to our world, and they in turn locate us in relation to theirs.

We are always told that Renaissance drama performed history as if it were contemporary, but these images render such a claim untenable. On the contrary, the examples we have considered provide a good index to the limitations of the imagination of otherness. Our sense of the other depends on our sense of its relation to ourselves; we understand it in so far as it differs from us, and conversely, we know ourselves only through comparison and contrast, through a knowledge of what we are not—we construct the other as a way of affirming the self. Anachronisms, then, far from being incidental or inept, are essential; they are what locate us in history, and the meaningful re-creation of the past requires the semiotics of the present. Indeed, the concept of anachronism may be considered essential to the very notion of historical relevance itself, which assumes that the past is in some way a version of the present.

We can illustrate this by looking ahead. We might expect that significant changes in the utility of anachronism as theater in the later eighteenth century and throughout the nineteenth century became increasingly concerned with realism and ultimately with historical accuracy. But in fact, anachronism and realism have more to do with each other than we are generally aware. For example, when John Rich produced *Henry V* at Covent Garden in 1761, he included a replica of the coronation of King George III, which had taken place earlier that year. This was so popular that it was subsequently included in *2 Henry IV*, *Richard III*, *King John*, again in *Henry V* five years later in 1766, and once again in *Henry V* as late as 1769.[4] Half a century later Shakespearean producers found the coronation of George IV in 1821 similarly relevant: Covent Garden mounted *2 Henry IV* with an elaborate replica of the procession and ceremony—the king had even permitted copies of the royal robes to be made for the spectacle. John Bull said of this that "a more splendid pageant never graced a Theatre," but complained about the presence in it of the Yeomen of the Guard because the order had not been founded until the reign of Henry VII, concluding that "a more glaring anachronism never slipped upon the stage."[5] As anachronisms go, this is certainly a minor one; but the Yeomen of the Guard were included at Covent Garden precisely because they *were* anachronistic—precisely because they had appeared not at the coronation of Henry V (or Henry VII) but at that of George IV. It is the accuracy of the contemporary pageant that establishes both the authenticity and the relevance of the performance; and the movement toward anachronism is also a movement toward both realism and history.

What, then, would happen if a Renaissance play, with its fluidity and anachronism, were put into one of Serlio's generic settings? Most Renaissance plays, after all, and all the ones we value most and consider most characteristic, are in mixed genres—as Sidney disapprovingly sums up the theater of his time, "neither right Tragedies, nor right Comedies, mingling Kinges and Clownes,...mongrell Tragicomedie."[6] Serlio's settings look very solid and consistent, and their genres are mutually exclusive. But even this is in certain ways an illusion. Figure 1.10 is Inigo Jones's Serlian setting for a court play called *Artenice*, performed in 1626. This elegant drawing has more relevance to the Peacham *Titus* sketch than is apparent at first glance. The play is one in which the queen is to perform, therefore Jones includes the aristocratic

*Figure 1.10*    Inigo Jones, setting for the Sieur de Racan's *Artenice* at Whitehall, 1626.

classical architecture and the open perspective of the Tragic Scene; but it is also a comedy, so it includes a merchant's house with its Italian Renaissance loggia; but the queen and her ladies play shepherdesses, so it includes the rustic huts and woods of the Pastoral Scene—it is a heroical-comical-pastoral. What this means is not that Serlio was conceiving of a drama that was generically pure, but that Serlio's settings were taken to be analytic, not descriptive. One thing we tend to forget is that even the purest of Renaissance tragedies would have appeared *to an audience* to belong to a mixed genre—to be a "mongrel tragicomedy"—because in performance it would have included comic or satiric *intermezzi* between the acts, and in England, some sort of jig at the end. As Serlio conceived them, the genres constituted not an idea about the necessary structure of plays, but an idea about the potentialities of theaters to realize the classic forms. And what the models then offered to someone like Inigo Jones was just the opposite of that rigid consistency we find in them: a very fluid set of possibilities.

I turn now to what is arguably the most far-reaching conception of theater the English Renaissance produced. Figure 1.11 is the titlepage to the Ben Jonson folio of 1616, engraved by William Hole, presumably to Jonson's specifications. On either side of a central cartouche stand the figures of Tragedy and Comedy. Below them are two scenes illustrating the ancient sources of drama, on the left the *plaustrum*, or cart of Thespis, with the tragedian's prize, a sacrificial goat, tethered to it; on the right a small amphitheater, labeled *visorium*, with a choric dance in progress. Above Tragedy and Comedy the third of the ancient genres, the satiric or pastoral, is anatomized: on the left a satyr plays a Pan's pipe, on the right a shepherd plays a shaum. Between them is a Roman theater, and above that, at the very top of the arch, stands Tragicomedy, flanked by the tiny figures of Bacchus on the left and Apollo on the right, the two patrons of ancient theater. Jonson's title page, with characteristic gravity, presents nothing so transient and particular as a scene from a play. It defines the drama in relation to its history and its kinds, and offers a set of generic possibilities.

This all seems distant, formal, quintessentially classical, and quite unlike the historical macaronic of the *Titus Andronicus* sketch. But look closely at the two plinths. The detail in Figure 1.12 is Thespis, the founder of tragedy, in his cart, a figure lost in antiquity and legend. But unlike all the other classic figures above him, he is in Jacobean dress, a modern playwright—Jonson himself—and clearly one of us. Figure 1.13 is the ancient amphitheater, labeled *visorium*. *Visorium* is not in fact the Roman word for amphitheater. It is not a classical Latin word at all, but (like the Rufia of Serlio's Comic Scene) is a Renaissance coinage. And the chorus that dances within it is, like Thespis, Jacobean. For the Renaissance classicist, the ancient world was our world, and anachronism was an essential element in the realization of the past.

Figure 1.11    Title page to Ben Jonson's *Workes*, 1616, engraved by William Hole.

Figure 1.12    Thespis in his cart, detail of 1.11.

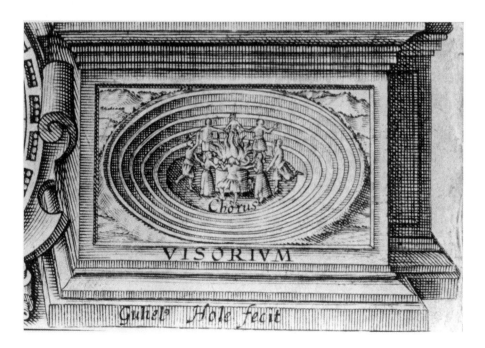

Figure 1.13    Choric dance, detail of 1.11.

To give a sense of the persistence of the generic assumptions, I turn now to a group of much later examples. Figure 1.14 is the frontispiece to *Julius Caesar* in the first illustrated Shakespeare, edited by Nicholas Rowe and published in 1709. Notice not just the architecture, which is perfectly logical for a Roman play, but also the symbolic monuments in the background. These come directly from Serlio's Tragic Scene of almost two centuries earlier, and serve to stamp the play as high tragedy. Comedy by this time had moved indoors, into drawing rooms and bedrooms, but for the artist, the generic assumptions were still operative. Figure 1.15 is the frontispiece to *Volpone* from the first illustrated Jonson, published in 1716. *Volpone* is largely an indoor play, but the illustrator has moved it outdoors, where it is recognizable not only as a city comedy, but as a generic one too; the private houses, shops and churches, and the closed perspective, all derive from Serlio's Comic Scene. And the pastoral too became a little neater, but its conception remained substantially unchanged. Figure 1.16 is the frontispiece to Rowe's text of *As You Like It*, 1709: a very up-to-date Orlando, Rosalind and Celia, but in a setting as old as the hills. There is, moreover, no particular scene from the play being illustrated here—the artist is illustrating the genre.

Let us turn now to another idea of drama. We may consider the action of a play as something separate from the form in which it is presented; and in this case, the fact that the play is a play is merely incidental. As an abstract proposition this sounds complicated, but all it means is that we may decide that the essential element in *Hamlet* is the story of Hamlet—as Aristotle said, it is the action, the plot, that is the essence of drama—and you can tell the story of Hamlet any way you wish, as a novel, film, opera, ballet: it will still be *Hamlet*. This may sound simplistic, but it is the view that illustrators, artists, and a large number of literary critics have most often adopted—basically, that the play is a story, or in more modern versions, a poem, or in postmodern versions, a text.

We may begin with an example contemporary with Shakespeare. In 1602 the most famous Renaissance pastoral drama, Guarini's *Pastor Fido*, was published in a magnificent edition with full page illustrations and copious explanatory notes. Figure 1.17 is one of the plates. What is depicted is not a scene from the play, but a conspectus of the events of a whole act; they are depicted, moreover, in the most traditional way, as if they were taking place simultaneously—the temporal progression of the action has been translated into a spatial one. This is the way epic poetry was illustrated in the period, and in this edition, with its critical commentary, the pastoral drama is dignified by being treated not as theater but as a classic text, just as Jonson was to do with his tragedy *Sejanus*.

Figure 1.14    Frontispiece to *Julius Caesar* in Nicholas Rowe's
edition of Shakespeare, 1709.

*Volpone or the fox.* Lud. Du Guernier inv. et Sculp.

Figure 1.15    Frontispiece to *Volpone* in Tonson's
edition of Ben Jonson, 1716.

Figure 1.16    Frontispiece to *As You Like It* in Nicholas Rowe's
edition of Shakespeare, 1709.

*Figure 1.17*    Giovanni Battista Guarini, *Il Pastor Fido*, 1602, frontispiece to Act 3.

In this example, the drama still consists of characters and action; it is only the contexts, temporal and theatrical, that have been removed. But the notion behind it has interesting consequences; because if we believe that a play really is a text, then its characters and action are no more essential to it than any other element of that text: in a poem, the characters are no more "real" than metaphor, imagery, rhetoric, even syntax, of which they all are, indeed, literally a function. It is generally claimed that the notion of a Shakespeare play as a poem, rather than as a theatrical event or a script, is a peculiarly modern one, a phenomenon of twentieth-century literary criticism, momentarily anticipated by Coleridge. But in fact, visual artists have been treating the plays in this way since the eighteenth century. For example, around 1790 Robert Smirke did a series of paintings for John Boydell's Shakespeare Gallery depicting the Seven Ages of Man from the "All the world's a stage" speech in *As You Like It*. Figure 1.18 shows the lover (he is composing his love poems beneath pictures of Cupid ruling the world and performing the balcony scene from *Romeo and Juliet*). This romantic youth is not a character in the play, he is part of a rhetorical exercise, one of Jaques's exempla for the sententious theme of his famous setpiece. Smirke here illustrates not the drama but the poetry, not the action but the language—we might even say not the play but the text. Shakespearean pictures of this sort grew increasingly common; and

Figure 1.18    After Robert Smirke, The Lover, from The Seven Ages of Man in *As You Like It*. From Boydell's *Prints...Illustrating the Dramatic Works of Shakespeare*, 1803.

far from being an invention of G. Wilson Knight, the notion that a Shakespeare play was not theater but poetry had become, by the early nineteenth century—by the time Coleridge had his proleptic critical intimation about it—really a commonplace of pictorial art. The visual arts are in this respect about fifty years ahead of the literary theorists: no critic before Coleridge conceives of Shakespearean texts in this way.

The work of Edmund Dulac offers another, even clearer example. Dulac was a prolific and popular illustrator of elegant editions of Shakespeare early in the twentieth century. Plate 1 shows his illustration for Ariel's song in *The Tempest* "Full fathom five thy father lies." Most of Dulac's illustrations are, like this one, representations of things that never happen in the play, but are only described or alluded to, sometimes merely as similes or metaphors—as elements, that is, of the verbal or poetic structure of the play, not of the plot or action. The drowned father depicted here is a fantasy, a figment like Jaques's Lover; Alonso is in fact perfectly safe, and appears on stage in the next scene.

The polar opposite of the notion that a play is a poem is one that ties the drama solidly to the particular, momentary and temporal—not to its characters but to its actors, not to its action but to its production. This is the concept anticipated in the fresco of *Oedipus* in the Teatro Olimpico, which is not simply a painting of a scene from the play, but a representation of a particular performance at a particular place and time. In this conception, the drama's reality is the reality of its presentation; this is how it is realized, made real. There is, of course, a long and distinguished tradition of theatrical portraiture, though it is curiously attenuated in Shakespeare's time. Let us look at some portraits of Shakespeare's colleagues in action, and consider the relation between the actor and the role. Figure 1.19 shows Richard Tarlton, the most popular Elizabethan clown before Will Kempe and Robert Armin, doing a characteristic performance. The actor here is identified with his role, but the role is generalized: this is not represented as a performance in a particular play or on a particular occasion; and the elaborate decorative frame, which firmly locates the image not on a stage but within a graphic or calligraphic context, is visually the most striking element of the picture. In contrast, Figure 1.20 is Robert Armin, the most famous clown of Shakespeare's company, probably the first Feste, probably the fool in *King Lear*, and, most tantalizing, the author of a play with the unpromising title *The History of the Two Maids of More-clacke*, which is a parody of *Hamlet*. (Though the surviving text is somewhat garbled and the play is admittedly not a masterpiece, it is—or ought to be—invaluable evidence for anyone interested in how Shakespeare appeared to his contemporaries. It is, on the contrary, totally ignored, which says something about how interested we really are in the historical Shakespeare.) Armin is represented here, on the title page of the first

Figure 1.19    Richard Tarlton, wood engraving after a contemporary drawing, from *Tarleton's Jests*, ed. J. O. Halliwell (London, 1844).

published version of his play, in his own role of John, a natural fool; but we know this only because we can tell by internal evidence that he played the part. The picture illustrates the play, and the character it depicts is named on the title page; but it is not identified as a portrait of the actor, and certainly not of the author.

Let us now consider a formal portrait. The solemn gentleman in Figure 1.21 is the most famous actor of the age, Edward Alleyn, creator of Tamburlaine and Doctor Faustus. The portrait makes much of his dignity but includes no allusion whatever to his profession. Faustus himself appears conjuring up a devil on the title page of the second quarto of Marlowe's play, shown in Figure 1.22. The magician is presumably being played by Alleyn, but if this is a representation of the great actor, there is no indication of the fact—all the reality is the reality of the role. Indeed, if we look for a portrait of an actor in a particular dramatic role in Shakespeare's time (rather than a generalized one, such as a clown), the closest thing we find is the manuscript illustration in Figure 1.23, the actor John Green in the role of Nobody in the comedy *Nobody and Somebody*. Green was with a troupe in Germany, where the painting was done in 1608, and he is identified in the manuscript. But

**THE**
**Hiſtory of the two Maids of More‑clacke,**

VVith the life and ſimple maner of Io н м
*in the Hoſpitall.*

Played by the Children of the Kings
Maieſties Reuels.

VVritten by Robert Armin, ſeruant to the Kings
*moſt excellent Maieſtie.*

*LONDON,*
Printed by *N.O.* for *Thomas Archer*, and is to be ſold at his
ſhop in Popes‑head Pallace, 1 6 0 9.

Figure 1.20    Robert Armin, *The History of the Two Maids
of More‑clacke,* 1609, title page.

even here, the picture alludes only to the character; this is presented as a
portrait of Nemo, Nobody, not of the actor John Green in a role.

Let us now look ahead. Plate 2 is Hogarth's great painting of Garrick as Richard
III, done around 1741. This role was Garrick's first real success, and the
painting conveys brilliantly a strikingly original conception of the character,
not the half comic machiavel of Shakespeare's text, but a figure of magnificent will and passionate intensity, satanic but also heroic and even glamorous.
A reader of the play may find this interpretation difficult to sustain—there is
a good deal in the text that contradicts it. Nevertheless, largely through the
combined efforts of Garrick, Hogarth, and perhaps most of all Hogarth as
engraver, it became the standard interpretation. The engraving made from

Figure 1.21    Portrait of Edward Alleyn (British school).

Figure 1.22 Faustus conjuring, from the title page of *Doctor Faustus*, 1620.

this painting was phenomenally popular, and for generations of English audiences, well into the next century, it was less Garrick in a particular role than a portrait of Richard III; so that in 1801 Charles Lamb could criticize the actor George Frederick Cooke for emphasizing the villainous and grotesque aspects of the part, elements that are certainly not underplayed in Shakespeare's text. We can see how much the interpretation exemplified in the Hogarth portrait owed to the artist rather than to the actor by looking at two other paintings of Garrick in the same role. These are for revivals, and Garrick is more than twenty years older, but his interpretation has not changed. The artists' interests, however, are clearly different from Hogarth's. Figure 1.24 is Nathaniel Dance's version. The intensity is still there, but it is conveyed now through the combined effects of terror and menace, and the romantic attraction of Hogarth's figure is quite gone. There is a rather fussy attention to costume, too, which seems to burden Richard here, rather than, as in Hogarth, to ennoble him and set him off. Plate 3 is Henry Fuseli's sketch of the same production. Fuseli has his eye on Garrick, but gives a quite different reading of the text: this is Richard as the traditional snarling machiavel.

All these representations of Garrick also involve a notion of historical representation, if only by implication—Fuseli alone presents Garrick's Richard

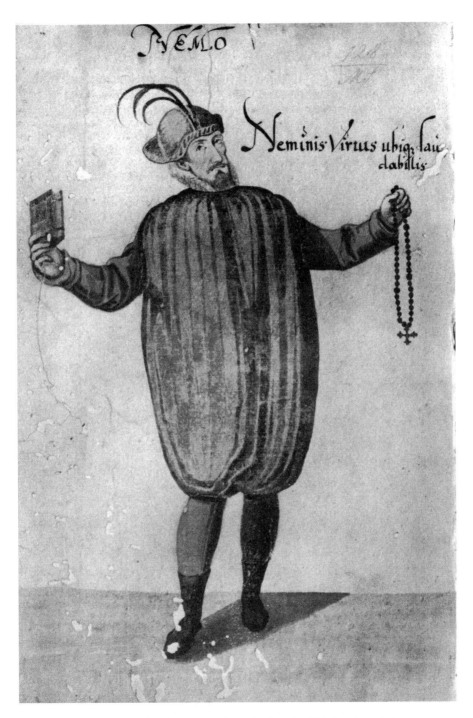

Figure 1.23    John Green as Nobody in the play *Nobody and Somebody*.
Watercolor drawing.

Figure 1.24    After Nathaniel Dance, *Garrick as Richard III*.

on a stage, in a scene from a play. Hogarth's and Dance's Richard is engaged in a real action, but though Hogarth depicts a minutely realized battlefield and Dance a landscape, neither removes the action from present time into history. Garrick had made a genuine attempt to return to Shakespeare's original texts, but he had no interest in returning the plays to either the world that generated those texts or the world represented in them: his Richard was neither Elizabethan nor fifteenth-century; his Shakespeare was contemporary.

This brings us to a final way we think of the reality of drama, as the reality of what is represented in it, the world of fact, behind the text, which the play brings to life. The days are long past when a book about the girlhood of Shakespeare's heroines could be taken seriously, but we still mine the plays for what they can tell us about social, cultural and political life in Renaissance England, assuming that they must reflect some reality beyond Shakespeare's imagination. It is especially difficult not to think of the history plays as versions of an ulterior reality, and our sense of British history is, in many cases, genuinely determined by Shakespeare. *Richard III* provides a good example: Shakespeare's play is based on blatant Tudor propaganda, but even if we are aware of the historical evidence that Richard was in fact a progressive and reasonably popular king, that there is no evidence that he had a hunchback, and that the evidence that he murdered his nephews is at best ambiguous, it would obviously be perverse to try to "correct" Shakespeare by reference to history. *Macbeth* offers a much more striking instance. How many of us are even aware that, historically, it was Duncan who was the usurper, his murder was a political assassination, Macbeth was a popular hero, and the legitimate heir to the throne was Lady Macbeth? Here Shakespeare's version of events has simply replaced history, probably irredeemably, for all but the most specialized of scholars. In such cases, the play becomes transparent, a glass through which we believe we see the past, or the culture, or the real life of the characters. For the Hamlet of Shakespeare's age, however, theater was not transparent but reflective, a mirror held up to nature, and what it showed was not the past but the present, not the other but the self.

# Two

## Staging Clio

How did history come to play so profound a role in determining our sense of Shakespeare? In 1859, Charles Kean presented his last Shakespearean spectacle in London, *Henry V* at the Princess's Theatre, the culmination of a long series of historical extravaganzas. Shakespeare's text, however, was not sufficiently historical for Kean, and he included a number of spectacular reconstructions of events and places that are only described or alluded to in the play, or, in some cases, that are not in the play at all, but only in the chronicles on which the play is based. The most lavish of the historical spectacles was devised for Henry's triumphant return to London after the victory at Agincourt, an event that is dispatched in ten lines of the Chorus's prologue to Act 5. In the physical, staged presence of Henry and his army, Kean reasonably enough found the Chorus redundant, and cut the ten lines to five.

But it was not only the introduction of historical episodes that anchored the play to history. Twenty years earlier, for a *Henry V* at Covent Garden, Macready had imported the figure of Time from *The Winter's Tale* to serve as the Chorus. Kean went a step further and reconceived the Chorus as Clio, the muse of History. The allusion to *The Winter's Tale*, however, was still palpable: at the opening Clio stood in a tempietto beside a broken column (Figure 2.1), "looking," as the *Saturday Review* said, "like a fine polychrome statue," and clearly recalling Mrs Kean's Hermione at the conclusion of Kean's *Winter's Tale* three years earlier. The interrelationships between history and romance are part of my subject, and as it happens, the inspiration for Clio was not entirely, or even primarily, textual: "Thus," Kean explained, "without violating consistency, an opportunity is afforded to Mrs Charles Kean which the play does not otherwise supply, of participating in this, the concluding revival of her husband's management"—history was also autobiography. The sentiment

*Figure 2.1*   Ellen Tree (Mrs Charles Kean) as the Chorus in *Henry V*. Watercolor.

was duly praised, but the innovation was only indifferently successful. Reviewers were unhappy with a female Chorus and saw in Mrs Kean's Muse the image suggested all too clearly by the production sketch in Figure 2.2, "a pantomimic fairy, summoning tableaux vivants from the midst of pasteboard clouds,...conjuring up visions and gliding mysteriously in and out like a spirit"—a muse who trivialized history instead of embodying it. Mrs Kean's Clio may stand as an introductory emblem of the problems of construing history as spectacle.[1]

The problems begin, however, with the very idea of construing history as drama, the notion that we can understand the forces that led to the deposition of Richard II, the Wars of the Roses, the Tudor revolution, by inventing dialogue for a few figures mentioned in the chronicles and putting them in dramatic situations. But the problem with this assumption is not that it is absurdly reductive: all history, as it undertakes to give a coherent interpretation of the past, is reductive. The problem is what it implies about drama: the logical corollary to it is that the reality of drama is not what it presents but what is represented in it, the world of fact, behind the text, which the play purports to bring to life—the true history of Henry V; not Shakespeare's poetry, but what really happened. Drama then becomes transparent, a glass through which we perceive the real, and is therefore logically

Figure 2.2    Ellen Tree (Mrs Charles Kean) as the Chorus in *Henry V*. Watercolor.

subject to any amount of revision to bring it into closer coincidence with that putative reality—hence Kean's historical interludes, designed to rectify Shakespeare's omissions.

I am concerned here particularly with the representation of history; but in this respect the history play is merely a special case illustrating a general tendency to locate the truth of drama in the life of its characters, whether historical or not, and to assume for them an existence before and beyond the play—the tendency enshrined in that Victorian classic to which I have already alluded, Mrs Cowden Clarke's *The Girlhood of Shakespeare's Heroines*. I have observed that we feel very far from this famous and influential work now, but we are not at all, in our critical and editorial practice, free of its assumption that the essence of drama is character, that characters have consistent psychologies determining their motivations, and that what we see of them is only part of a larger whole that exists outside the play. Shakespeare's knowledge of human psychology has always been claimed to be beyond praise, but in fact the plays have always required a good deal of help in this department, and much of the commentary in editions since Pope's has been concerned with explaining why the characters say what they say, justifying lines that look obscure or inconsistent, when they have not been editorially "rectified" by outright emendation. The character is thus conceived to be something different from the lines, prior to the dialogue we are elucidating or emending.

This seems to us a logical and perhaps even inevitable procedure (the characters, after all, are surely supposed to behave like people), and I am not arguing that we are necessarily wrong to do it, only teasing out its implications. But there are alternative editorial and critical possibilities: we might, for example, think of characters not as counterfeit people, but, as I have already suggested, simply as part of the text. This in fact is the original meaning of the word *character*: both a written account of a person, and the letters—characters—in which the account is written. When I was a student learning how to deal with literary texts, William Empson at one blow vanquished the sentimental philistines by pointing out that we cannot dispose of a passage like the famous aphorism in *King Lear* "As flies to wanton boys are we to the gods:/ They kill us for their sport" (4.1.36–7) by remarking that it is uttered by the crude and prosaic Gloucester, not by the sensitive and perceptive Cordelia or Lear. Plays, Empson observed, have linguistic and poetic structures, and characters are not independent of those structures. The notion that the gods make fools of us is one that runs throughout *King Lear*, and is not dependent on the view of any particular character.[2] Characters, that is, are not people, they are elements of a linguistic and poetic structure, lines in a drama, and more basically, words on a page. This argument had, for some graduate students at Harvard in the 1950s, a wonderfully liberating effect.

It is, of course, very difficult to think of character in this way, to release character from the requirements of psychology, consistency and credibility, especially when those words on a page are being embodied in actors on a stage, who have to make their roles psychologically believable. Nevertheless, a large number of Renaissance dramatic characters, from the genuinely complex, such as Malvolio or Sir Epicure Mammon, to the patently parodic Lussurioso, Black Will, Sir Beauteous Ganymede, and the immortal Supervacuo, have natures that are defined, encapsulated, determined simply by the most basic of linguistic and textual structures, their names. The role of Hamlet may be said to imply an inner life—the character certainly claims to have one—but to attempt to understand Malvolio through notions of psychology, of stimuli, acculturation, development, childhood trauma, is defeated at the outset by the mere *dramatis personae*: Malvolio, or Volpone, or Subtle are not what they are because of something in their childhoods; what they are is their names, which constitute, in the most platonic way, their essence.

This might, of course, turn out to be true for all characters if we knew more about the psychology of playwrights. The fact that Shakespeare had a son named Hamnet and a younger brother named Edmund has not been lost on psychoanalytic critics. Drama was obviously undertaking to free itself from the constraints of nomenclature when it started calling its characters names like Claudius instead of names like Everyman. But even here, the effects of nomenclature are often more textual than dramatic. For example, Claudius has no name in *Hamlet*; nowhere in the dialogue, in any of the three texts, is he ever called anything except the king. He is also called "King" throughout the speech headings, and none of the original texts includes a cast list. The name Claudius appears only once, in the second quarto and folio texts, in the stage direction for his first entrance: "Enter Claudius King of Denmark"; it is never used again. For audiences experiencing whatever text, he has no name; indeed, even for actors working from the first quarto he will be only the king. Why then is he Claudius? For whose benefit was the name included in that single stage direction?

The answer can only be, for Shakespeare's. What constitutes the real or essential in Shakespeare, then, necessarily involves us in a notion of Shakespeare's own psychology, for if characters like Hamlet or Falstaff appear to be prior to, or to have a life outside, their plays, they have never seemed prior to or beyond the reach of the playwright's imagination—they are, indeed, the witnesses to Shakespeare's genius. There *are* people who say "I can't see how someone as uninteresting as Shakespeare can have written *Hamlet*," but this is in the interests of producing another Shakespeare—Bacon, Marlowe, the Earl of Oxford, someone whom they *do* find interesting. Baconians, Oxfordians and Shakespeareans are identical in the sense that we all have, almost from the beginning, constructed a personality and a history for Shakespeare that accounts for the plays. And how we think about Shakespearean drama is deeply implicated in what we think about Shakespeare—criticism, biography and history have always been profoundly interdependent. Even good poststructuralists who believe they have disposed of the author are probably reading Shakespeare in collected editions that are organized chronologically; our sense of the plays, whether we like it or not, is imbued with a notion of the development of the playwright's mind and art. In contrast, Shakespeare's editors throughout the seventeenth century organized their collected Shakespeare generically, Comedies, Histories, Tragedies—chronology, development, even within the categories, was irrelevant: Hemming and Condell, the editors of the first folio, are the true poststructuralists. The basic circularity of our system is indicated by the fact that *The Tempest* became, for critics, a much better play when Edmond Malone decided, in 1812, that it was not one of Shakespeare's earliest works, as had previously been assumed, but his last. Neither of these propositions is correct, but they indicate the extent to which critical history is a function of biography. Constructing a life for Shakespeare out of the evidence of the plays has been a thriving critical enterprise since the late seventeenth century—this is a matter to which I shall return in Chapter 3.

The representation of history, however, is only incidentally tied to biography. Granting that the interests of writers, whether historians or fabulists, are a function of their lives, history makes its claims as an account not of the historian's psyche but of a world of events and facts, and Shakespeare's history plays certainly purport to represent history, not Shakespeare. Nevertheless, as I have observed, our sense of British history is, in many cases, genuinely determined by Shakespeare. The historical Richard III was neither as ugly nor as malevolent as Shakespeare's machiavel; but even if we are aware of the distortions of Tudor propaganda, there is clearly no way of "correcting" Shakespeare by reference to history, and historians who undertake to return to the sources and depict a different Richard are considered revisionists. In *Macbeth*, as we have seen, Shakespeare's version of events gets everything backwards: historically, Duncan was the usurper, his murder was a political assassination, Macbeth was a popular hero. Shakespeare has effectively replaced history.

In fact, Shakespeare apparently saw nothing about history that required any special fidelity to the chronicler's version of events—he is not, that is, notably more faithful to his sources in the history plays than he is in the tragedies or comedies. But in imagining Shakespeare, history came, by the nineteenth century, to play the greatest role; so that even plays that take place in no clearly recognizable era, say *King Lear* or *The Winter's Tale*, were felt to show us how life was lived in some specifically definable past. In producing such plays, the age almost invariably felt it necessary to invent a milieu and a historical moment, to locate the drama firmly in the world of historical and geographical fact. The drama's verisimilitude was thus provided by history; and the increasing pressure toward archeologically accurate productions of Shakespeare is one of the most characteristic intellectual phenomena of the nineteenth century. The most enlightening works on the sources and implications of this movement are Martin Meisel's brilliant and compendious (and seriously under-appreciated) *Realizations*, and Richard Schoch's exemplary *Shakespeare's Victorian Stage*,[3] books that have served as my guides throughout this investigation.

Let us recall the *Titus Andronicus* sketch of *c.* 1595, reproduced in Figure 1.6. The costumes provide some sense of period, but primarily they are designed to give a clear indication of every character's role: Roman general, generic queen, Elizabethan guardsmen are grouped together in an integral, though anachronistic, stage picture. Now let us move a century forward. Figure 2.3 is the plate illustrating Shakespeare's *Henry VIII* in Rowe's edition of 1709, the first illustrated Shakespeare. It shows the king, Cardinal Wolsey and three

Figure 2.3    Frontispiece to *Henry VIII* in Rowe's Shakespeare, 1709.

courtiers. The king is authentically Tudor, but the Cardinal and the courtiers come from the world of 1709. Nothing has changed since 1595 in the conventions of costuming.

Despite the radical anachronism, drama here is clearly at the service of history: Henry VIII has to be recognizable as Henry VIII, not simply as a generic king; and through an allusion to Holbein's famous portrait of the monarch the costume makes the point—history lies, as I have remarked, precisely in the anachronism. But the world of the play is modern; except for the Roman plays, to which I shall return, Shakespearean productions throughout the eighteenth century were presented in contemporary dress. If a medieval milieu was required, it was provided by the scenery. Zoffany, for example, provided a medieval chamber for Garrick and Mrs Pritchard in *Macbeth*, but clothed them in modern dress (Plate 4). Odd as this looks to us, it is a reasonable enough conception—people do, after all, sometimes live in old houses. What such a production says is that the characters are just like us; Shakespeare is faithful not to history but to nature, and nature is not confined by historical eras. For comparison, Figure 2.4 is an eighteenth-century *Romeo and Juliet*: Spranger Barry, the most popular Romeo of the mid-century, and Isabella Nossiter in 1759. This looks, even to a twenty-first-century eye, entirely convincing; and yet there is nothing at all about it to suggest Renaissance Verona—it is quite Mozartean.

Archeological realism, with its assumptions about the possibility of re-creating the past, is in its way equally romantic, but it starts from a different set of assumptions. I begin with an egregious modern example. Figure 2.5 is a postcard, purchased in Verona, of the authentic Romeo and Juliet. The house is, or at least for the purposes of the tourist industry is claimed to be, the Capulet family house; it has only one balcony, so that must be Juliet's balcony. There is, in fact, nothing at all inaccurate about the costumes of the figures, but their cartoon prettiness gives the show away. This is the alliance of archeology and romance, with romance firmly in control.

How did we get to such an image as a version of Shakespeare? For my purposes, the great intellectual moment comes in 1786, when John Boydell, engraver and publisher, alderman, sherriff, and ultimately Lord Mayor of London, announces his intention of commissioning a series of paintings illustrative of Shakespeare, and the creation of a Shakespeare Gallery, which he duly opened in Pall Mall. The grand motive behind this scheme was to found and encourage a native British school of history painting—this was considered the most serious kind of painting, but it had found few practitioners and fewer patrons in England. British artists, Boydell believed, had the technical skill and the genius necessary to compete with history painters on the continent; what they lacked was a suitable subject. And the one national

Figure 2.4    Spranger Barry and Isabella Nossiter in *Romeo and Juliet*, 1759.

Figure 2.5    Romeo and Juliet, picture postcard c. 1975.

subject about which there could be no disagreement, Boydell concluded, was Shakespeare.

There is a breathtaking leap of faith in Boydell's proposal, which I believe has gone unnoticed. It is the illogical leap from Shakespeare as a national subject to Shakespeare as a historical subject. As a way of regarding Shakespearean drama, this is radical and unprecedented. Beside it in the history of Shakespearean criticism, Coleridge's claim that the plays are poems, Lamb's that they are unproducible, Wilson Knight's that they are extended metaphors, pale into insignificance. All at once, in 1786, Shakespeare stopped being our contemporary and became history.

I confess that I have, in the interests of my narrative, simplified and dramatized the transition from Shakespeare-as-nature to Shakespeare-as-history. The proposal to make Shakespeare the universal theme for British history painting originated not with Boydell but with a bookseller who was one of his associates: the idea was doubtless somewhere in the air. The first Shakespeare production in Elizabethan dress had already been presented three years earlier, John Philip Kemble's *Hamlet*, and Talma was about to launch a similar movement on the Paris stage. It was clearly an idea whose time had come.

*Figure 2.6*    Garrick as Hamlet.
Mezzotint after a painting by Benjamin Wilson.

History painting as Boydell and the age conceived it implies relatively little in the way of archeological fidelity, though it does tie the expression of noble sentiments and general truths to particular historical moments or incidents, and therefore consistency and credibility are central to it. Garrick's *Hamlet*, in the painting by Benjamin Wilson in Figure 2.6, conveys superb conviction, not least because the great actor looks at home in his clothes, and not as if he is wearing a costume. But this was just the sort of thing that Boydell and his artists rejected, as, increasingly, did producers of the plays. Kemble's 1783 Elizabethan *Hamlet*, in Figure 2.7, actually is not very Elizabethan, though it certainly is not eighteenth century either. In this case, moreover, the historical accuracy has to do with Shakespeare's history, rather than with Hamlet's, and this is an important distinction to which I shall return; but the significant point here is the urge to remove the play from the world of present time. We can see a new idea of history in operation, too, Enlightenment history having

*Figure 2.7* John Philip Kemble as Hamlet,
Covent Garden, 1783.

its effect on theater: such a production says that history is not cyclical but linear and progressive; the events of the past are in the past—we are not versions of the Romans or Elizabethans, however much we may learn from them. The underlying assumption is that the universal and general are historical, or to put it another way, that what we learn from history are universal truths. Of course if the truths are really universal, we ought to learn them from contemporary examples as well as from ancient ones, but the contemporary was felt to be a distraction, too localized and trivial.

All this naturally posed considerable difficulties for theatrical producers, because the most powerful source of authority in Shakespearean production lay not in history but in the theatrical tradition itself. Eighteenth-century reviewers and critics regularly built their reviews around comparisons of present productions with earlier ones; Betterton's performances were still being used as guides in the late eighteenth century (Betterton died in 1709), and since Betterton had begun his career acting under Davenant, and since Davenant had worked with actors who had worked with Shakespeare, there seemed—and indeed in some ways there really was—a genuine link, through the performing tradition, with Shakespeare's own stage.

It is precisely that sense of the authority and autonomy of the theater that breaks down at the end of the eighteenth century. And along with this, we have to remember two important points about English theater history: first, that throughout the eighteenth century and well into the nineteenth, most theater in England was Shakespeare. By far the greatest number of productions were revivals of Shakespeare plays, and new plays comprised only a very small part of the repertory. Actors got their training and much of their experience playing Shakespearean roles, and audiences were thoroughly familiar with the Shakespeare canon. Second, however, and paradoxically, Shakespeare has never constituted a classic drama for the English in the way that Corneille, Racine, Molière have been classics for the French. Shakespeare has nearly always been our contemporary in one respect, which has to do not with the costumes but with the texts of the plays, which have been, as we have seen, almost from the beginning, endlessly rearranged and rewritten. No French producer, at least until well into the twentieth century, ever changed a word of *Le Cid* or *Phèdre*, but Nahum Tate's *King Lear*, with its notorious happy ending, is in no way uncharacteristic of British theatrical practice. Historically, very little authority in Shakespearean drama has ever been felt to inhere in the texts. The eighteenth century saw the most serious critical effort before the present to establish an authoritative text of the plays— it succeeded, of course, only in establishing a new authoritative text every ten years or so, but the goal, however elusive, was stabilization and critical consensus. That, however, was for scholars; it never occurred to any actor or producer that those were the versions to perform, rather than the revamped versions of Tate or Cibber. For the theater, the reality of Shakespeare was the reality of performances; and when Garrick advertised that his *Macbeth* was being presented for the first time "as written by Shakespeare,"[4] he was making a revolutionary claim.

The claim, however, was not even approximately true; Garrick merely took as his working text Theobald's recent "authoritative" edition of the play rather than the standard stage version of Davenant. But he cut more than 10 percent of it, while incorporating some of Davenant's most popular bits for the witches, and wrote a whole new dying speech for himself as Macbeth. The original text, in fact, was only marginally more satisfactory to Garrick's sense of the play than Davenant's had been. Why then the claim of authenticity? Twenty years earlier a producer could have expected to attract audiences by advertising a whole new *Macbeth*, bigger and better. Garrick's invocation of the author to confer authority on the production revives Davenant's claim of a direct line to Shakespeare himself, but it now insists that the line descends not through the text or some personal knowledge of the man, but through the stage: Garrick asserts, in effect, that through his theatrical genius he knows what Shakespeare would have written had he been alive to revise.

When Boydell delivered Shakespeare over to both art and history, however, he was assuming that the authority of the plays derived not from the text or even from the author, but from the subject matter; that the texts were triumphs of representation, and what was authentic in them was what was represented. The Shakespeare Gallery was a failure, but its influence was immense; it contributed, through engraved versions of the paintings, an iconography of Shakespearean drama that remained standard for more than a century. The iconography was not invariably historical: it included the extraordinary fantasies of Henry Fuseli. But the stage followed Boydell's principles, not his artists' practice, and increasingly in the nineteenth century theater was seen as a kind of history painting. The classic accounts of this movement are in W. Moelwyn Merchant's book *Shakespeare and the Artist* and Martin Meisel's *Realizations*. I shall confine myself to a single well-known example, first noticed by the Shakespearean editor George Steevens in 1790, just at the time when Boydell's project was getting under way.

Steevens called attention to an interesting anomaly in the illustrations for Rowe's Shakespeare of 1709, the first with illustrations. These are characteristically based on contemporary performance practice, even in cases where the play had not been performed for decades. But the frontispiece to *Coriolanus* (Figure 2.8) is a properly classical rendering of the moment in Act 5, scene 3, when Coriolanus receives his mother, wife and son at his encampment outside Rome, and they plead with him not to destroy the city. Figure 2.9, however, shows how the eighteenth century performed its *Coriolanus*: this is James Quin, the major tragedian before Garrick, and the exotic costume derives from Italian opera—Figure 2.10 is Garrick in the same outfit for a play called *The Roman Father*. Roman plays, as I have observed, were the exception to the eighteenth-century rule that Shakespeare was to be presented in modern dress. Steevens observed that Rowe's illustration comes directly from Poussin's famous painting of the scene as described in Plutarch, reproduced in Figure 2.11 from an early eighteenth-century engraving. But both the illustration and the painting differ from the text in one very important respect: Shakespeare has Coriolanus seated, holding court like a monarch— he is compared to the enthroned Alexander.[5]

We now move ahead to the turn of the century. Plate 5 is the plate from Ackerman's *Microcosm of London*, published in 1808, showing the interior of the Drury Lane Theater; Thomas Rowlandson did the figures, A. C. Pugin the architecture. The scene in progress is again *Coriolanus* V.3, and it is again the scene as imagined by Poussin. Rowlandson, like Rowe's illustrator a century earlier, went to Poussin for his inspiration: the compositions are almost identical—but not quite. The plate must also represent a production, because the setting has now had introduced into it, directly behind the standing figure of Coriolanus, an armchair. This is a prop required only for the actual

*Figure 2.8*    Frontispiece to *Coriolanus* from Rowe's Shakespeare, 1709.

*Figure 2.9*    James Quin as Coriolanus.

staging of the play, and it means that the famous artist, the great history-painter, has now become an authority not only for illustration but for stage practice as well.

This, however, is art, not archeology. The first historically correct productions are those of Charles Kemble, based on the researches and designs of J. R. Planché; playbills and advertisements for such productions always stress, as a primary attraction, the historical seriousness of the event. The playbill for Kemble's 1823 *King John*, an originary moment for stage archeology, declares that the play will be presented "with an attention to costume never before equalled on the English stage. Every character will appear in the precise habit of the period, the whole of the dresses and decorations being executed from indisputable authorities"—the authorities cited are not textual but material, visual, documentary: tomb effigies, royal seals, manuscript illuminations. Figure 2.12 shows the models Planché provided for Shakespeare. These, and others like them, were the basis for the costumes of Kemble's *King John*, and

Figure 2.10    Garrick in William Whitehead's *The Roman Father*.
From *The Universal Magazine*, February 1750.

again of Macready's in 1842; the costumes remained unchanged because they stamped the productions as authentic. This is what Planché did to theater. It also gives a striking sense of what the attractions of theater were now conceived to be. The underlying assumptions here are not new. Kemble and Planché reassert Addison's claim a century earlier, in his treatise *On Medals* (1708), that the truth of history is not to be found in literature, which is too prone to misrepresentation on the one hand and misinterpretation on the other, but in objects, the material remains of culture. And Addison, in his turn, was refining and refiguring the ideology of a long line of Renaissance humanist antiquarians. But it is a new idea for the stage, and the most striking part of it is the assumption that the truth of both theater and drama is the truth of history.

In the case of the history plays, archeology conferred more benefits than merely consistency and authenticity. As Richard Schoch, in *Shakespeare's Victorian Stage*, has shown, it conferred political benefits too, and for all parties. For Whigs, the Middle Ages were the source of all the ancient rights and liberties to which every Englishman was entitled; for Tories, they embodied the traditions and precedents which only the conservative party could maintain. It is both ironic and characteristic that the first Shakespeare production to

Figure 2.11    *Coriolanus*, engraving after Nicholas Poussin.

Figure 2.12    J. R. Planché, royal effigies from the reigns of Henry II, Richard I
and King John, from his *History of British Costume*, 1847.

claim serious historical credentials should have been Kemble's *King John*, a history of the reign that does not mention Magna Carta. Kemble apologized in his playbill for Shakespeare's omission, though, like Macready and Charles Kean after him, he stopped short of rectifying it. Herbert Beerbohm Tree, in his 1899 *King John*, finally supplied the lack with a sumptuous pantomime of the king signing the elusive document. Three brief scenes from this production were the first bits of Shakespeare ever recorded on film; they include a wildly melodramatic death scene, but not, unfortunately, the interpolated Magna Carta pantomime.

Tree's mute addendum does more than "correct" Shakespeare; it acknowledges an increasing problem in both producing and elucidating the plays: the fact that Shakespeare's concerns often simply do not coincide with ours. The Magna Carta scene therefore rectifies not only history, but Shakespeare's imagination as well. It is characteristically Victorian, however, only in its bias toward historicity; the attitude it reveals toward the text is as old as Shakespeare himself. Think back to the *Spanish Tragedy* woodcut and the *Titus Andronicus* drawing (Figures 1.5 and 1.6), with their revised personnel and confected dialogue. Such images, no less than Beerbohm Tree's pantomime, confront us with the question of what the real play is, of what we mean by "Shakespeare."

Soon enough after Kemble's *King John*, everything became history—tragedies and even comedies were increasingly located securely within historical time. And in this respect plays like *Hamlet* and *Macbeth* pose real problems: what time do you locate them in? John Philip Kemble's 1783 Elizabethan *Hamlet* was a logical start, placing the play in the world of Shakespeare and his audiences; but for directors like Charles Kemble and Charles Kean, the logic was irrelevant: the history had to be not Shakespeare's but Hamlet's, not the history of the play but that of its fictive hero—it was not until a century later that William Poel would realize the possibilities inherent in Kemble's historical experiment, and undertake to present the plays as Shakespeare's audiences would have seen them. As the nineteenth century began, however, *Hamlet* became a generalized medieval world, though the prince himself retained Kemble's Elizabethan puff-pants until the 1830s, when Charles Kean introduced the more properly medieval tunic. Delacroix's famous series of illustrations for the play is obviously influenced by an older stage practice— the only time he saw the play was apparently on a visit of the English players to Paris in 1827. The lithograph in Figure 2.13, done almost twenty years later, is his version, or recollection, of the bedchamber scene, just before the murder of Polonius. Notice the medieval queen: her son's costume is a good two hundred years later than her own. Talma, in Paris (Plate 6), was by this time being both archeological and literalistic: his Hamlet is a sixteenth-century German university student.

*Figure 2.13*    Eugène Delacroix, The Bedchamber Scene in *Hamlet*, lithograph (1844).

There is no reason to feel that Talma's décor is more appropriate, more authentic, than Delacroix's—Shakespeare, even in the history plays, is full of anachronisms—but the trend in both production and illustration was increasingly toward Planché's and Talma's kind of literalism; and the text, in this enterprise, often had to be radically adjusted. Charles Kean's productions by the mid-century were setting a standard of accuracy that was to remain normative for the next fifty years. We have looked at his *Winter's Tale* and *Henry V*; Figure 2.14 is the banquet scene in his 1853 *Macbeth*, a detailed and historically informed architectural reconstruction, in which Banquo's ghost, which has just appeared beside a massive column, looks quite dwarfed. The costumes, however, posed the same problems that Ellen Terry noted in the authentically ancient Sicilian costumes for Kean's *Winter's Tale* (in which she made her debut at the age of nine as Mamillius): Kean's Macbeth, in Figure 2.15, is all shaggily medieval, but Mrs Kean, despite her authentic Scottish apron, refused to play Lady Macbeth without petticoats, just as she had refused to wear Hermione's third-century drapery without the same properly decent undergarments.

*Figure 2.14*    Setting for Charles Kean's *Macbeth*, Princess's Theatre, 1853.

To get a sense of what the movement toward history meant in practice, let us consider three versions of the play scene from *Hamlet*. First, in Plate 7, are the English Players in Paris in 1827, the production that so impressed Delacroix. It had, to judge from the print, a rather generalized Renaissance feel; certainly the sense of anachronism in the décor is much less pronounced than it is in Delacroix. This lithograph obviously influenced Daniel Maclise when he did his celebrated painting of the scene in 1842 (Figure 2.16). The setting is much more detailed, and all the details are appropriately medieval; though the whole composition has the air of a Victorian house-party

*Figure 2.15*    Charles and Ellen Kean
as Macbeth and Lady Macbeth, 1853.

theatrical, if a rather sinister one. The illustrator Edwin Abbey, at the end of the century, sets his *Hamlet* in a barbaric Viking décor (Figure 2.17): this, he believed, was the real thing. He explained that he wanted to "represent the plays not as they might *poetically* be conceived, but as they might *actually* have happened." *Hamlet* had, of course, precisely been poetically conceived, and did not and could not ever actually have happened. What is being realized here, however, is not the text, but the history behind the text, a history that has had to be invented. All three of these realizations are felt, in their periods, to be historically correct.

This is not to say that theatrical archeology was without its critics; reviewers regularly poked fun at Charles Kean's pedantry even as they praised his command of spectacle, and he was frequently criticized for sacrificing so much of the text to the scenery. ("As for the acting," *The Times*

*Figure 2.16*   Daniel Maclise, the Play Scene from *Hamlet*.

*Figure 2.17*   Edwin A. Abbey, the Play Scene from *Hamlet*.

*Figure 2.18*    Henry Irving as Macbeth, 1888.

said of his *Tempest*, "there is not very much room for it.") Sir Henry Irving's famous *Macbeth* of 1888, with Ellen Terry as Lady Macbeth, prompted the following observation:

> Archeological correctness has, of course, been studied in this revival, and we are assured that the British Museum and all known authorities on archeology have been laid under contribution for correct patterns of...the eleventh century. Shakespeare wrote *Macbeth* in the language of the sixteenth century, and in the most important point of all, therefore, every performance of the play...must be grossly inaccurate. The real Macbeth of the eleventh century would certainly have had some difficulty in expressing himself in Shakespeare's English, nor can we suppose him to have been in the habit of speaking blank verse. These matters, however, are overlooked by the archeologists, who devote their best efforts to the cut of the clothes and the arrangement and number of the buttons worn by the different characters.[6]

Figure 2.19    John Singer Sargent, Ellen Terry as Lady Macbeth.

This sounds persuasive, a refreshing return to the text; but in fact *The Times* is being quite as literalistic as Irving's archeologists. Surely no theatergoer can have been conscious of a contradiction between eleventh-century costumes and sixteenth-century English; even in the sixteenth century people did not talk in blank verse (though *The Times* appears to believe that they did)—if the play had been *Hamlet*, doubtless the complaint would have been that the prince was not speaking Danish. A critic who came much closer to

*Figure 2.20*    Edward Gordon Craig, King Lear in the Storm.

the point in his comments on Irving's *Macbeth* was Oscar Wilde. In this
production Ellen Terry wore an extraordinary costume covered with beetles'
wings; she was painted in the role by Sargent, crowning herself (Plate 8)—
a bit that Terry and Sargent had added to the play: it appeared in neither the
text nor the production. Wilde observed that

> Judging from the banquet, Lady Macbeth seems an economical housekeeper and
> evidently patronises local industries for her husband's clothes and the servants'
> liveries, but she takes care to do all her own shopping in Byzantium.[7]

This was the most carefully researched and historically accurate *Macbeth* ever undertaken; but to Wilde—surely an educated eye if there ever was one—the costumes looked inconsistent. This does not mean they *were* inconsistent; it only means that few of even the most sophisticated spectators will have been sufficiently qualified as archeologists to tell. Irving's own costume as Macbeth (Figure 2.18) is unquestionably conceived for a play located in medieval Scotland. But Figure 2.19 shows that the decor suggested to Sargent a world elsewhere, utterly exotic: the scene might be a Moorish fantasy.

I began with Mrs Kean as Clio, a touchstone for Shakespeare as history. Viewed from where we stand, theatrical archeology seems an attempt not to make Shakespeare more real or more accurate, but more manageable and comfortable, even sentimental; to locate the plays at a safe distance, so that they became like household bric-a-brac, souvenirs of a colorful past. The new technology of film, moreover, could not only realize that past, but preserve and reproduce it to order. The theater's reaction, when it came at the turn of the century, was to try abandoning history entirely. Edward Gordon Craig, Ellen Terry's son and a phenomenally inventive theorist and stage designer, summed up the possibilities of an abstract theater with the brilliant sketch for *King Lear* in Figure 2.20: text, history, biography, even character, are all but irrelevant here; the artist rules, and the stage has a life of its own.

1. Edmund Dulac, illustration for 'Full fathom five thy father lies . . .', *The Tempest*, London, 1908. Stanford University Library.

2. William Hogarth, *Garrick as Richard III*. Reproduced by permission of the Board of Trustees of the National Museums and Galleries on Merseyside (Walker Art Gallery, Liverpool).

3. Henry Fuseli, Garrick as the Duke of Gloucester in *Richard III*. Kunsthaus Zurich.

4. Johann Zoffany, Garrick and Mrs Pritchard in *Macbeth*. Garrick Club, London.

5. Thomas Rowlandson and A. C. Pugin, Drury Lane Theatre, with *Coriolanus* in progress. From Ackermann's *Microcosm of London*, 1808.

6. Talma in *Hamlet*, color engraving. By permission of the Folger Shakespeare Library.

7. The English Players in the Play Scene from *Hamlet*. Color lithograph. Courtesy of Bibliothèque Nationale de France, Paris.

8. John Singer Sargent, Ellen Terry as Lady Macbeth. Tate Gallery.

9. Henry Wallis (1830–1916), A Sculptor's Workshop, Stratford-Upon-Avon, 1617. From the RSC Collection with the permission of the Governors of the Royal Shakespeare Company.

10. The Flower Portrait, Shakespeare Birthplace Trust, Stratford-Upon-Avon.

11. Jim Dine, costume design for
Puck, for the Actors' Workshop
production of *A Midsummer
Night's Dream*, San Francisco,
1966. Watercolor and pencil.
The Museum of Modern Art,
New York. © 2003 Jim
Dine/Artists Rights Society
(ARS), New York. Digital Image
© The Museum of Modern Art/
Licensed by Scala/Art Resource,
NY.

12. Jim Dine, costume design for
Titania. Watercolor and
pencil. The Museum of Modern
Art, New York. © 2003 Jim
Dine/Artists Rights Society
(ARS), New York. Digital Image
© The Museum of Modern
Art/Licensed by Scala/Art
Resource, NY.

13. Quentin Metsys the Younger,
Elizabeth I (The Sieve Portrait).
Pinacoteca Nazionale, Siena.

14. Giulio Romano, Jove seducing Olimpia. Fresco in the Palazzo Tè, Mantua.
Copyright Scala/Art Resource New York.

15. Giulio Romano, Cupid and Psyche in bed. Fresco in the Palazzo Tè, Mantua. Copyright Scala/Art Resource New York.

16. Giulio Romano, *Ceres*. Louvre, Paris. Copyright Scala/Art Resource New York.

# THREE

## History and Biography

Historical representation is a significant issue in the case of Shakespeare himself. The history of Shakespearean portraiture as a means of getting at the real Shakespeare provides a remarkable index to a whole complex of critical attitudes.[1] To start at the beginning, there are only three portraits of Shakespeare with any claim to authenticity. These are the engraving on the folio title page, the memorial monument to Shakespeare in the Stratford parish church, and a painting now called the Flower portrait; I shall for the moment consider only the first two, and return to the third.

Martin Droeshout, the engraver of the title page portrait (Figures 3.1a and 3.1b show the title page opening of the first folio), was a young and inexperienced artist. At the time of Shakespeare's death, in 1616, he was fifteen years old; he was twenty-two when the folio was published, and this image is, so far as we know, his first commissioned work. If the engraving derives from a portrait made from life, the portrait must have been done by someone else and Droeshout must have done his work many years later. In fact, Droeshout's presence on the title page of this elaborately produced, very expensive book is a real puzzle. The portraits included in similar volumes in the period are for the most part provided by a small group of very accomplished artists: Simon van de Passe, Cornelis Boel, William Hole, Robert Vaughan, William Marshall.[2] Moreover, the very fact that the portrait is on the title page is puzzling. Normally the author's portrait would be facing the title page, as a frontispiece—especially if it is engraved, because it was quite difficult to combine typesetting and engraving on the same page. If the portrait had been a woodcut, there would have been no problem: woodcuts could be printed on the same press with, and at the same time as, type. Engravings, however, require a quite different printing technique, and the Shakespeare title page therefore would have had to go through two separate

# To the Reader.

This Figure, that thou here ſeeſt put,
   It vvas for gentle Shakeſpeare cut;
VVherein the Grauer had a ſtrife
   with Nature, to out-doo the life :
O, could he but haue dravvne his vvit
   As well in braſſe, as he hath hit
His face ; the Print would then ſurpaſſe
   All, that vvas euer vvrit in braſſe.
But, ſince he cannot, Reader, looke
   Not on his Picture, but his Booke.

                                        B. I.

Figure 3.1a    Title page opening of the First Folio.

Figure 3.1b    Title page opening of the First Folio.

processes. The usual way of dealing with this, if one wanted an engraving on the title page, was to engrave the whole page, as was done for Ben Jonson's *Workes* (1616), Drayton's *Poly-Olbion* (1613), Chapman's Homer (1611/1616), and innumerable other large, important, expensive books. The publishers of Shakespeare were making trouble for themselves.

Opposite the title page, where the frontispiece would normally go, is a poem in large type—this, technically, is the frontispiece. The poem is addressed To the Reader, and urges us to ignore the portrait:

> This figure, that thou here seest put,
> > It was for gentle Shakespeare cut;
> Wherein the graver had a strife
> > With Nature, to outdo the life:
> O, could he but have drawn his wit
> > As well in brass as he hath hit
> His face, the print would then surpass
> > All that was ever writ in brass.
> But since he cannot, reader, look
> > Not on his picture, but his book.

"Look/ Not on his picture, but his book": the poem construes the portrait and the book as alternatives, or even adversaries. The poem is signed only with the initials B.I., and has always been credited to Ben Jonson. I do not doubt that this is correct, but it is worth remarking that there are other people in the period with the initials B.I. or B.J. Indeed, Jonson's other dedicatory poem in the volume is signed in his characteristic way, "Ben: Ionson," and Jonson did not subsequently include the poem anywhere among his works. In effect, he disowned the poem in the course of dismissing Shakespeare's portrait.

Still, whatever the portrait's quality, it is the closest we can come to a piece of hard evidence about what Shakespeare looked like, so let us consider what it tells us about how Shakespeare was imagined in 1623, seven years after his death. Since the folio was published by Shakespeare's lifelong friends and associates as a memorial to their most famous colleague, we would expect the frontispiece to show him as those who were closest to him wanted him to be remembered.

The most striking feature of the face is the very high, slightly bulging forehead. The nose is long, the eyes large, the lips fairly full, with the lower lip perhaps protruding a little; but if any part of the physiognomy is to be taken as distinctive, it will be the forehead. The sitter wears a full-dress Jacobean costume, with an unadorned flat starched collar instead of the more usual, and more elaborate, ruff—the technical term for this is a band, and in most portraits, if the sitter is a gentleman, it appears edged with a good deal of lace. This, then, is the outfit of a prosperous man, but one who is in no way flashy. No jewelry is visible. The Shakespeare represented here is serious, solid, unostentatious. The implications of the portrait become a little clearer if we compare it with other frontispiece portraits of writers. Figure 3.2 is the poet and playwright George Chapman in 1616. His head is in the clouds, and behind him is even the hint of a halo. No costume whatever is visible. Figure 3.3 is Ben Jonson, dressed with great simplicity but crowned with the poet's laurel wreath. Shakespeare in the Droeshout engraving is not being presented as a poet or intellectual, but rather as a solid citizen.

Figure 3.2   George Chapman, from *The Whole Works of Homer, Prince of Poetts*, 1616.

The Stratford funeral monument (Figure 3.4) was sculpted by Gerard Janssen the younger, unlike Droeshout, a well known artist with a significant body of work behind him, including the tomb of Shakespeare's patron the Earl of Rutland. The Shakespeare monument was presumably begun after the playwright's death in 1616, and must have been in place by 1623, since it is alluded to in the prefatory verses to the first folio. This shows an older and stouter Shakespeare than Droeshout's, but the same distinctive forehead appears. And unlike the engraving, it does allude to the playwright's craft:

Figure 3.3    Ben Jonson, from the second edition of the *Works*, 1640.

his left hand rests on a sheet of paper, his right hand holds a pen. He wears a plain collar and cuffs, a doublet, and a simple sleeveless jacket. Beneath the bust are inscribed two elegies. The first, in Latin, compares Shakespeare to Nestor, Socrates, and Virgil; the second, in English, can find no terms of comparison for him, but declares that nature died with him—the conceit had earlier been used for Raphael's epitaph. Janssen's sculpture itself, however, makes no such claims for its subject. The figure is serious and dignified; he looks academic or clerical. He writes; he is not crowned with laurel or surrounded with a glory, and nature is in no danger from his mortality. Both the Droeshout and Janssen portraits are remarkably unsentimental versions of the man, and not, so far as we can tell, especially idealized.

Now let us turn to the Chandos portrait (Figure 3.5). This hangs in the National Portrait Gallery in London (it is, indeed, the originary national portrait, number 1 in the Gallery's catalogue), and it has for about three centuries been the standard portrait of Shakespeare—it and the folio engraving are the two portraits that everybody recognizes at once as

*Figure 3.4*    The funeral monument to Shakespeare,
Holy Trinity Church, Stratford-Upon-Avon.

Shakespeare, though they do not look at all alike. I am not concerned at the moment with the authenticity of the Chandos portrait; what matters is that from the mid-seventeenth century on, *but not earlier*, it has been thought to represent Shakespeare. The high, vertical forehead of the two undoubted portraits is missing; this sitter's forehead slopes back. The face is rounder, the eyes much smaller, and the features look rather Mediterranean: commentators generally characterize the complexion as swarthy (one late

nineteenth-century critic accounted for its distinctly un-English aura by identifying it as Shakespeare in his makeup for the role of Shylock). The dress is
very plain; notice, however, the gold earring, oddly out of character with the
sobriety of the rest of the costume: a little high style has crept in, though
whether louche or courtly is unclear.

Figure 3.5    The Chandos Portrait.

The reason the Chandos painting has been the standard portrait of
Shakespeare since about 1660 has more to do with provenance than with
physiognomy; I shall return to this issue. But the image's problematic
character as a version of the greatest playwright was evident from the first,
and almost at once adapters and copyists set out to rectify its defects—
implying thereby, of course, that it is the copy that is the true original. An early
revisionary example is the Chesterfield portrait (Figure 3.6), probably by a
Dutch painter working in London in the 1660s. It has significantly anglicized
the swarthy sitter, who is now an aristocratic bibliophile in his elegant

library—this is Shakespeare the playwright who never published his plays, for whom plays were not books. The portrait revises much more than its sitter's appearance. Gerard Soest, who came to London in 1656, derives from the Chandos portrait a romantic English gentleman (Figure 3.7). The features are more refined than those of the earlier examples we have looked at—significantly more refined, in particular, than those of the Chandos portrait on which it is obviously based (in keeping with its new refinement, the troublesome earring has been removed)—but the hairstyle now is especially notable. Carelessly windblown, it is the hair of a Cavalier gentleman; whereas the clothes, on the contrary, represent a real attempt at historical accuracy. In her brilliant book *Seeing Through Clothes*, the costume historian Anne Hollander remarks that in movies set in the past, the clothing will often be archeologically accurate, but the hairstyles tend to be strictly contemporary. This is necessary if the stars are to look glamorous.[3] The Soest portrait is the first in which Shakespeare starts to look glamorous.

The Chandos portrait has had a very long reach. When Garrick posed for Roubiliac's statue of Shakespeare, the stance was the actor's but the head was based on the painting (Figure 3.8). The painting in Figure 3.9, *Shakespeare as*

Figure 3.6    The Chesterfield Portrait, c. 1660–70,
attributed to Pieter Borseller.

*Figure 3.7*    The Soest Portrait, c. 1660–80,
attributed to Gerard Soest.

*a Boy of Twelve*, by the late Victorian painter James Sant, is one of the Chandos portrait's oddest derivatives. It is a piece of pure Victorian kitsch, but it has a curious resonance, and the attitude it embodies is not a Victorian innovation. It began almost as soon as the Stratford memorial effigy was dry. Milton in 1631 could imagine hearing, in *L'Allegro*, "Sweetest Shakespeare, fancy's child/ Warble his native woodnotes wild": Shakespeare the artless free spirit, at home with fancy and nature; perhaps most important, Shakespeare the child. Think of the unostentatious solid citizen of the Droeshout engraving and the Stratford bust; think of Ben Jonson's famous poem on his famous friend, or, indeed, of Milton's own handsome and dignified elegy on Shakespeare written for inclusion in the second folio—"so sepulchred, in such pomp dost lie/ That kings for such a tomb would wish to die." Nothing in any of these suggests "fancy's child" as an appropriate epithet for the playwright. The sentimentalization and miniaturization are part of a bucolic and disarming fantasy: Shakespeare is, after all, not only the author of the sweet and fanciful *Midsummer Night's Dream*, but of *Richard III*, *Macbeth*, *King Lear*, *Coriolanus*, daunting models for even so self-confident a poet as Milton. It is, however,

Figure 3.8    Louis Roubiliac, Shakespeare.

a fantasy that starts very early—"O Sweet Master Shakespeare," says a character named Gull in a satiric academic play called *The Return from Parnassus* in 1600, "I'll have his picture in my study."[4] Sweet master Shakespeare becomes the contemplative muse: Milton in 1631 treats this as already a commonplace, and it continues to be an integral part of the legend.

Figure 3.9   James Sant, *Shakespeare as a Boy of Twelve*.

But why, given the unquestionable credentials of the folio frontispiece and the Stratford bust, did the Chandos portrait, which looks so little like them, become the standard portrait of Shakespeare? Its claims lie not in its dubious physiognomy, but, as I have indicated, in its provenance. It is said to have belonged to Sir William Davenant—this is plausible, though it cannot be ascertained—and subsequently it belonged to Thomas Betterton, the greatest Shakespearean actor of the Restoration. Davenant is a central figure in the creation of Shakespeare's history, and whether he owned the painting or not, it is significant that the history constructed for the portrait begins with him. He was, for thirty years or so, the most important theatrical entrepreneur in

England. He was the only person licensed to produce theatrical entertainments during the Commonwealth, and at the Restoration his royal patent explicitly stipulated that he re-create a Shakespeare appropriate to the modern stage. He idolized Shakespeare, and amassed a huge collection of Shakespeareana, presumably with the portrait as its centerpiece; he believed that Shakespeare's mantle had passed to him. He is reported to have claimed to be Shakespeare's godson, though there is no other evidence that he was, and it is in fact quite unlikely—Shakespeare's will records small bequests to various associates including a godson, but Davenant is not among them. Long after his death he was said even to have claimed to be Shakespeare's illegitimate son. This is first reported by John Aubrey as a joke of Davenant's: he "would sometimes, when he was pleasant over a glass of wine..., say that it seemed to him that he writ with the very spirit that did Shakespeare, and seemed contented enough to be thought his son."[5] Aubrey, noting that the story casts an unflattering light on Davenant's mother, considers the joke in poor taste. It is only reported as fact when, nearly a century after Davenant's death and half a century after Aubrey's, an eighteenth-century antiquary without a sense of humor takes it seriously. Neither of these claims, it should be noted, can be traced directly to Davenant: both are stories told about him, and they have more to do with establishing Davenant as a link to Shakespeare than with either of the playwrights themselves.

The claim that Davenant had an intimate connection with Shakespeare derives from the fact that his father was an Oxford innkeeper—the inn, at least, is verifiable (it survives, and is now a Pizza Express). Davenant either said, or was said to have said, that Shakespeare stayed at his father's inn on his trips between London and Stratford, thereby giving him access either to the baptismal font or Mrs Davenant's favors, depending on which elaboration of the story you believe. Hard evidence for Shakespeare's patronage of the Davenants' inn is once more nonexistent; the story is again first recorded by Aubrey. But, to return to the portrait, even if it is true that Shakespeare stayed with the Davenants when William Davenant was a child, does that make him a reliable witness as to Shakespeare's appearance? Davenant was born in 1606; he was seven when Shakespeare moved permanently back to Stratford in 1613, and ten when Shakespeare died. The most we can say is that it may be true that Davenant thought he had a picture of Shakespeare.

It is clear that the real force of the Chandos portrait's claims lay, for the seventeenth and eighteenth centuries, in its association specifically with the theatrical tradition: with Davenant, who, whether or not he knew Shakespeare as a child, was the link between the old stage and the new; with Betterton, the greatest Shakespearean actor of the age, who lived on into the eighteenth century. Indeed, early commentators insist on the theatrical connection, ascribing the portrait to an actor in Shakespeare's company named Joseph

Taylor, or even to the star of the company Richard Burbage. These figures provided the direct connections with Shakespeare's stage that Davenant himself could not quite offer; the portrait's authority rests on mystical assumptions, but they are no less powerful for that.

To the eighteenth century, the acting tradition was the clearest and most meaningful link with Shakespeare. At the same time, the age saw a considerable rise in the status of the theatrical profession as a whole—we have seen that by the 1660s portraitists were turning the Chandos Shakespeare into a painting of a prosperous gentleman, bibliophile or cavalier. However authentic the original portrait might be, it nevertheless would not do for Shakespeare any more. More profound transformations were to follow.

For example, consider Garrick's first great success, *Richard III* in 1740. We have already considered Hogarth's great painting of the production, in Chapter 1, Plate 2. Figure 3.10 is a detail of the head, taken from the engraving by Hogarth himself, issued in 1745, shortly after the painting was exhibited. For comparison, Figure 3.11 is an eighteenth-century engraving of the Chandos head, used as the frontispiece to Bell's Shakespeare published in 1774: versions like this were regularly reproduced, until the early years of the twentieth century, as the Chandos portrait. My point here is not that Garrick has made himself up to look like Shakespeare (though of course he may have done so, just as he posed for Roubiliac's statue of the playwright), but that the age's conception of Shakespeare grows increasingly theatrical—the similarity to an idealized Chandos head may well be Hogarth's idea rather than Garrick's. Figure 3.12 is the engraver John Mortimer's illustration, not of a scene from a play, but of a bit of Shakespearean musing, "the poet's eye in a fine frenzy rolling," as described by Theseus in *A Midsummer Night's Dream.* The date is 1775, and this is the same romanticized Chandos head from the side (including even the earring), turning Theseus' exemplum into a piece of Shakespearean autobiography.

But something beside theatricalism and romance enters conceptions of Shakespeare as the eighteenth century progresses. In the portraits as in the drama, it is history, initially, as we have seen, in the fairly oblique form of oral traditions recorded and recounted long after Shakespeare's death by antiquarian gossips. By about the middle of the century, however, *evidence* has started mysteriously to appear. For example, the Shakespearean editor Lewis Theobald claimed to have discovered three manuscripts of a lost Shakespeare play called *Cardenio.* We know that such a play really did exist: Shakespeare wrote it in collaboration with John Fletcher; it was produced in 1613, and appears under both playwrights' names in the Stationers' Register. Theobald shortened, revised and adapted the play, which he produced (unsuccessfully) under the title *The Double Falsehood* in 1727, but he never published the original, and none of the manuscripts has survived. It is now generally agreed that

Figure 3.10    Engraving after Hogarth, *Garrick as Richard III* (detail).

this was not a hoax: Theobald would not have known of the Stationers' Registry entry, which is the only reference to a Shakespearean connection with the play; the three manuscripts almost certainly existed. But the impulse not to leave the play as Shakespeare left it, to take possession of it, revise and refurbish it, characterizes the history of Shakespearean texts from the beginning. (Indeed, it continues to do so: Gary Taylor has now refurbished *The Double Falsehood* in an attempt to transform it back into *Cardenio*.) We have always been eager for evidence about Shakespeare, but we also want to be firmly in control of what the evidence tells us.

If Theobald's manuscripts were authentic, however, fictitious ones were appearing with such regularity as to constitute a genuine symptom of the intellectual pathology of the age. The Shakespeare forgeries of William Henry Ireland came at the end of a century whose literary monuments include Chatterton and Macpherson. The forgers moved, moreover, from imaginative re-creations to actual documents—Ireland produced not only a new Shakespeare play, *Vortigern*, but also mortgage deeds signed by the playwright, and a letter to Anne Hathaway enclosing a lock of his hair, which he begs her to perfume with her kisses. These forgeries, like most such productions, were

Figure 3.11    Frontispiece to Bell's Shakespeare, 1774.

almost immediately detected, and indeed, Ireland admitted them with some pride, and produced a genealogy purporting to show his descent from Shakespeare, thereby implying that he was entitled to write new Shakespeare documents. However zany the enterprise, Ireland's impulse is not entirely eccentric. It may be taken as a genuine expression of the age as a whole, which increasingly wants a Shakespeare grounded in fact, historically authentic. What Ireland is doing is inventing an archeology for Shakespeare.

Figure 3.12    John Mortimer, The Poet.

The next step is predictable. In 1849, in Mainz, Germany, Shakespeare's death mask appeared (Figure 3.13). Notice the finesse of the features: it is, commentators observed, a truly aristocratic face. Nothing in it suggests the common player or the poacher from Stratford. What is more to the point, nothing in it suggests the jowliness and the high vertical forehead of the Stratford monument, which would be the logical place to go for a death mask if you were setting out to invent one: this deceased's forehead slopes back.

The death mask is, again, a romanticized version of the Chandos portrait, Shakespeare the aristocrat and intellectual, precisely analogous to the substitution of Bacon for Shakespeare in the same period. Both have more to do with fantasies about Shakespeare at the age of twelve than with the sort of attempt to reconstruct missing pieces of evidence that Theobald's *Cardenio* and Ireland's *Vortigern* represent. Plate 9 shows the fantasy in action: in 1857, eight years after the death mask surfaced, Henry Wallis produced this painting of Gerard Janssen carving the Stratford funeral monument practically *in situ* (Holy Trinity, Stratford, is in the background), and using the death mask as his model.

At about the time the death mask appeared, an interesting painting of Shakespeare came on the English market (Plate 10). This is the Flower portrait,

Figure 3.13    The Shakespeare Death Mask.

so called from the name of its Victorian purchaser. Its early pedigree is unknown, but it is inscribed with Shakespeare's name and the date 1609, and it bears a direct and obvious relationship to the Droeshout engraving. Straightforward and unromantic, it is a persuasive painting, though its aura of age is partly contributed by the fact that there is a fifteenth-century Flemish painting underneath it. Its claim to authenticity has been further eroded by a chemical analysis, which has detected in it a type of black paint not in use until the eighteenth century. This persuaded David Piper that the portrait is a forgery, but the evidence is not quite as conclusive as it sounds: old paintings were often revised by later hands, just as old plays were.

It now seems most likely that the Flower portrait is not the original of the folio title page, but a painting based on it. Nevertheless, it is a knowledgeable painting, more knowledgeable about Shakespeare than the Chandos portrait: it contradicts the Chandos in a significant detail, realizing and preserving one tiny item from our small store of physical information about the man himself. Shakespeare's hair was light brown—not black, as the Chandos sitter's is. We know this is correct because the hair on the Stratford monument, which was originally polychromed, was described as auburn.[6] This must be right: the Chesterfield and Soest portraits, painted within living memory of the playwright's death, and when the monument was not yet whitewashed, also correct the color of the Chandos portrait's hair (everybody seems to have known what color Shakespeare's hair was except Davenant). If the Doeshout engraving is a portrait of Shakespeare, the Chandos sitter is somebody else.

Postmodern or not, we are the true heirs of a very old tradition. When Samuel Schoenbaum set out to write the definitive modern biography of Shakespeare, he began with a volume called *Shakespeare's Lives*, which systematically, masterfully, dismantled two centuries of romantic narratives about the playwright. This was followed by the real thing, *William Shakespeare: A Documentary Life*. Documents provide for us the irreducible minimum of fact. Such a historical argument is our own kind of romanticism. Schoenbaum finally produced the documents that Theobald and Ireland, and in the mid-nineteenth century John Payne Collier wanted so badly to find, and ended by inventing. I think we instinctively understand the motives behind a documentary life, and our age as a whole, concerned as it is on a megalomaniac scale with information retrieval, can hardly pretend to question its value. Nor shall I. But what is it that we want out of a likeness, or a biography? Do we really believe that getting back to the hard evidence, the documents, the facts, the undoubted portrait, is getting back to the real person? The mind, the character, the personality, are expressed in the plays and poems, not in the portraits or the facts. And appropriately, then, the closest we can come to an authentic physiognomy is not the painting certified by Davenant and

Betterton, or the posthumous tomb sculpture, or the nineteenth-century death mask, but precisely the title page of the book that claims to preserve "the true original copies"—and thereby answers Jonson's oppositional poem by insisting that to look on the picture *is* to look on the book: the plays *are* the portrait, and any true original is bound to be a copy.

# Four

## Magic and History

I

We now consider the interrelationships of script, performance, text and interpretation in the particular example of *A Midsummer Night's Dream*. I begin with a debate between criticism and performance as modes of interpretation, and go on to consider the play as a historical subtext for several other kinds of performance.

At a strange moment in *A Midsummer Night's Dream*, the play reaches out beyond its fiction to invoke the reigning queen as an etiological principle. Oberon explains to Puck:

> That very time I saw (but thou couldst not),
> Flying between the cold moon and the earth,
> Cupid all armed: a certain aim he took
> At a fair vestal, thronèd by the west,
> And loosed his love-shaft smartly from his bow
> As it should pierce a hundred thousand hearts.
> But I might see young Cupid's fiery shaft
> Quenched in the chaste beams of the watery moon;
> And the imperial votress passèd on,
> In maiden meditation, fancy-free.
> Yet marked I where the bolt of Cupid fell:
> It fell upon a little western flower...
> The juice of it, on sleeping eyelids laid,
> Will make or man or woman madly dote
> Upon the next live creature that it sees.    (2.1.155ff.)

Elizabeth's virginity accounts for the power of the little western flower, but her own authority is assured by the fact that she alone is untouched by the force it represents. In remaining safe from Cupid's fiery shaft, she has released into the play's world an embodiment of unbridled and arbitrary sexual passion.

I shall return to this moment, but I want to start by observing that despite the fact that at the center of the play Shakespeare has placed a principle of indiscriminate lust, the editorial tradition has been quite uniform in denying that there is any sexual complexity beneath the comic surface of *A Midsummer Night's Dream*. Even Peter Holland's admirably far-ranging and subtle introduction to the new Oxford edition warns us that "the innocent tradition of *A Midsummer Night's Dream* as the school-play Shakespeare *par excellence* does not need subverting." Nevertheless, the dark side of the play has surfaced fairly regularly in the performing tradition of the past thirty years, most notably in Peter Brook's famous, dazzling, radically destabilizing production of 1970, but even earlier in, for example, John Hancock's landmark production at the Actors' Workshop in San Francisco in 1966, with settings and costumes by Jim Dine, which took seriously the fact that Theseus is a warrior and Hippolyta both an Amazon and the spoils of his victory, not a romantic heroine but a captive enemy. Hancock brought her on stage in the opening scene in a cage, dressed in a tiger skin, snarling and delivering her romantic lines with heavy sarcasm from behind bars. The production also brought to the surface the play's view of sexuality as a universal and basically anarchic motivation, epitomized in a rainbow-colored Puck (Plate 11), swinging about the stage on a pink heart-shaped trapeze, and by Demetrius, who wore an electrified codpiece, which lit up whenever it was stimulated by some erotic innuendo in the text, and thereby made manifest a significant and generally suppressed dimension of the play's language. This in itself represented a significant suppression, because in Dine's original costume design, it was Titania's genitals that were electrified (Plate 12): was San Francisco in 1966 not yet ready for female sexuality? Gender was, in any case, fairly fluid in the production: Helena was played, for no apparent reason, by a six-foot-four man in drag.

Comedies, we are always told, are plays that end in marriages; but in Shakespeare's case this is not quite correct. The more characteristic Shakespearean ending comes just before the wedding, sometimes with an unexpected and dramatically unnecessary delay, as in *Twelfth Night* and *Love's Labour's Lost*. Shakespeare takes quite a dark view of life after marriage—the plays that continue after the accomplishment of the comic ending, with the older generation defeated and the lovers happily united, are *Romeo and Juliet* and *Othello*. Perhaps Shakespearean comedy is comic precisely because it ends where it does, just before the wedding. The few Shakespeare plays that treat what happens after marriage, *Hamlet*, *Macbeth*, *King Lear*, *Cymbeline*, *The Winter's Tale*, scarcely provide optimistic models. *A Midsummer Night's Dream*, it is often claimed, was written to celebrate a wedding, though no one has succeeded in finding the wedding. Still, it concludes on the eve of three fictive marriages, and therefore would hardly be expected to probe the dark side of its subject; but perhaps the relentlessly festive view most productions and commentators have taken of this comedy is more a function of what audiences, readers and critics have wished to ignore than of Shakespeare's way of fulfilling his putative commission. For a theater (and a society) as concerned with cuckoldry as the Elizabethans', no wedding was without its ominous overtones, and plays like Much Ado About Nothing and All's Well that Ends Well seriously question the claim implicit in their titles that marriage constitutes a happy ending. Are Claudio and Bertram really all that those wronged paragons Hero and Helena deserve, the best that exemplary women can hope for?

Indeed, if we take the play's celebratory aspects seriously and consider it in the context of traditional epithalamia, the ambiguous and enforced quality of the festivities unexpectedly becomes more rather than less striking. We tend to ignore how one-sided the triumph represented in the classic nuptial was, a victory for the husband with the bride as the prize. Ben Jonson, in a note to his wedding masque Hymenaei, explains that "the bride was always feigned to be ravished from her mother's bosom...because that had succeeded well to Romulus, who by force gat wives...from the Sabines," and Jonson's epi-thalamion, like its classic model in Catullus, describes the wedding night explicitly as a rape. In both poems the groom's anticipated pleasures are paralleled by the bride's fears. Spenser, in his Epithalamium for his own marriage, analogizes himself to Jove. His bride, however, is not Juno but Maia or Alcmena; the divine model for marriage is not a union with the queen of heaven, but rape, or adultery—or, alternatively, it is total impotence: the bride is also compared to Medusa, the beautiful woman transformed into a monster the very sight of whom turns men to stone. The wedding, for all these celebrants, includes its essential component of violence and danger. The ambivalence of the marriage celebration is even clearer in Catullus, who includes an overtly homosexual past for the bridegroom. The abandoned slave boy who has shared his bed desultorily serves sweets to the other slaves at the wedding feast. Nor is it clear that the competing passion is really in the past: "They say that you, perfumed bridegroom, are unwilling to give up your old pleasures, but (the poet urges him) abstain." Perhaps, analogously, the intensity of A Midsummer Night's Dream's focus on the arrangement (and rearrangement) of marriages reveals, more than anything else, how arbitrary the arrangements are on which the order of society depends, and how ambiguous their success is bound to be.

The arbitrariness and ambiguity are embodied in the play's persistent rep-resentation of magic as an utterly erratic but nevertheless indispensable element in the process of getting society's erotic arrangements right. Puck is the principal agent of Oberon's magic: Figure 4.1 shows a Renaissance Puck, not only mischievous but overtly sexual, a priapic satyr. This is the Puck Peter Holland chose for the striking cover of his Oxford edition, and it is the Puck of Shakespeare's world; the play reads and performs rather differently from "the innocent...school Shakespeare *par excellence*" if we keep this sort of Puck in mind. (The cover has since been replaced by the publisher with something more modest.) Oberon's magic has everything to do with sex, and without

Figure 4.1    A seventeenth-century Puck.
The volume first appeared in 1624.

magic, the play says, people fall in love with inappropriate people, or with people who do not love them, violate their vows, and are mere pawns of the patriarchal system. But if magic liberates lovers from the tyranny of paternal authority, it is also the instrument of a much larger patriarchal order, not at all liberating but ultimately controlling.

The notion of magic as an erotic control mechanism is most overtly expressed in The Tempest, in which Prospero's art is employed to produce the most literally farfetched of suitors for Miranda, the only appropriate husband her father can imagine, the son of his arch-enemy. And of course Egeus, the father whose will is overruled by the civil authority of Theseus, is perfectly justified in asserting, as Brabantio does at a similar moment in Othello, that his daughter has been taken from him by witchcraft—the more so since Oberon's magic could just as easily have worked in Egeus's favor, making Hermia transfer her affections from Lysander to Demetrius, the suitor of her father's choice. The patriarchy of the nuclear family is subverted here by the dual patriarchy of the state and of nature, the authority of Theseus on the one hand and Oberon on the other. But the issue of parental intransigence and thwarted love nevertheless remains, returning even as part of the wedding celebrations, in the parodic form of Pyramus and Thisbe.

Consider the play's magic, the little western flower. The enabling factor in its power to induce love is provided by a figure outside the drama's fiction: the magic works because of Queen Elizabeth's programmatic virginity. I have already quoted the passage describing the flower's etiology, which is solidly based on Elizabeth's personal mythology. In Figure 4.2, engraved after a miniature by Nicholas Hilliard, she wears the crescent moon of Diana in her hair, signifying her chastity. The imperial votress is protected by Diana from the wound of Cupid: in this allegory, Elizabeth's politic refusal to marry, her rejection of the happy ending of comedy, is not an act of her will but a divine defense of the freedom of her mind—an allegory that in fact comes very close to the political reality. But the principle of virginity thus placed at the center of the culture has also resulted in the creation of the little western flower, the agency of indiscriminate lust—the creation of the libido as a free radical.

The myth of the little western flower suggests that the play presumes, as a norm, a libidinous economy that is disrupted when Cupid's arrow misses its mark. But the economy does not in fact tend toward the social arrangements comedy is always said to assert—toward marriage, monogamy, the nuclear family. There is no lover presumed by Cupid's arrow; its wound produces only an infinite potential for infatuation, madly doting as a condition of life. Nor does the magic significantly alter the erotic conditions of the play's world: with or without the juice of the flower, people fall in love with inappropriate objects, or with people who do not love them. But

*Figure 4.2*   Detail of a memorial engraving by Francis Delarem
(c. 1617) of Queen Elizabeth wearing a crescent moon in her hair.

the fact that Elizabeth's commitment to virginity means that men can be *made* to betray their loves and women can be *made* to love asses, does have a significant resonance in the larger economy of a play nominally about sorting out society into suitable and mutually satisfactory marriages.

What is satisfactory about the play's marriages? Figure 4.3 is the earliest illustration for the play, the frontispiece to Nicholas Rowe's edition of 1709. The central figures are Oberon and Titania facing each other down, but they also clearly serve as models for the military duke and his Amazon bride. *A Midsummer Night's Dream* opens with the preparations for that royal wedding. As Louis Montrose, in a pioneering essay on the play pointed out, if we press even slightly on the two principals, the ominous overtones are immediately apparent.[1] In the mythological story, Theseus' marriage to Hippolyta follows his abandonment of Ariadne on Naxos, his betrayal of the lover who enabled him to destroy the monstrous Minotaur. As for Hippolyta, she is, as the Hancock production correctly presented her, not a romantic heroine but the spoils of war. In most sources (though not in Chaucer) it is not even Theseus who defeats her, but Hercules, who then gives her to Theseus as a gesture of friendship, the woman as the ultimate token of male bonding. Plutarch doubts this story, but is no less persuaded of the ominous character of all Theseus' relationships. "His womanishness"—that is, his interest in women—"was rather to satisfy lust than of any great love."[2] Shakespeare's source, indeed,

Figure 4.3    Frontispiece to *A Midsummer Night's Dream*
in Nicholas Rowe's Shakespeare, 1709.

has traditionally provided subjects for tragedy rather than comedy. The offspring of the marriage is Hippolytus—his name alludes to the manner of his death, "killed by horses," and Hippolyta's name is a back-formation from his. So Theseus' bride has no identity except through her son, who himself has no identity except through his death. Behind this story is the story of Theseus' subsequent marriage to Phaedra, sister of his previous lover Ariadne, a marriage that is, in both classical and Elizabethan law, incestuous, which is followed by Phaedra's uncontrollable love for her stepson, resulting in his revulsion from all women, and ultimately in both their deaths. This, indeed— not the romance of young love but the uncontrollable, destructive and incestuous nature of passion—is the central element in the myth.

The royal wedding, the comic conclusion, then, looks forward to adultery and a double incest, and on the part of its issue Hippolytus, to a compulsive flight from sexuality; which might provide us with another way of looking at the vestal queen Elizabeth's repudiation of love, her "maiden meditation, fancy free." And looking backward, behind the happy nuptial is not only Theseus' past history with women, but more particularly the defeat of the Minotaur, issue of the bestial lust of Queen Pasiphaë for a bull—an infatuation universally decried by the ancient writers, but with the direct precedent of Jove's seduction of Europa in the form of a bull, the foundational myth of the settlement of the European continent.

Titania's love for the ass-headed Bottom is easy to sentimentalize by turning Bottom into a big Stieff animal; but in the play its comedy is an aspect of its eroticism—it repeats the lust of Pasiphaë and makes of the Minotaur a love object. It also brings into the connubial life of the play a whole range of what, in polite Elizabethan parlance, is called "disorderly love," invoking the concept of buggery in both its legal senses, what we would divide into bestiality and sodomy. Peter Holland assures us that the Elizabethans did not think about sex at this point,[3] but such a claim is at best wishful thinking. Figure 4.4 is Henry Fuseli's late eighteenth-century vision of the scene, openly sexual, and a sufficient indication that the play's sexuality is not an invention of the last thirty years. Titania's love affair with Bottom is literally preposterous—his arse/ass is his head; he has in front what should be behind. This love affair, moreover, is imposed on her by her husband; if it is intended as a model for the indiscriminate profligacy of woman's sexuality, it is even more a model for the construction of the female libido by the male, a construction that is here specifically a function of marriage, the husband's way of punishing and controlling his wife.

The marriage of the king and queen of fairyland is in every sense a model for the play's erotic world. The mortal and fairy worlds are, indeed, connected precisely through their erotic interest in each other. Titania charges Oberon with having been Hippolyta's lover, Oberon accuses Titania of betraying him

Figure 4.4    Henry Fuseli, Titania and Bottom. Engraving by G. Rhodes after
Henry Fuseli's painting for Woodmason's Shakespeare Gallery, 1793–94.

with Theseus—the latter flirtation is entirely in character for Theseus, but the accusation is significant because it constitutes one more revelation by Oberon of his own cuckoldry.

Cuckoldry and adultery, however, are normative here, simply the stuff of marriage. The real issue, the efficient cause of Oberon's rage, is Titania's refusal to give up to him

> A lovely boy, stol'n from an Indian king—
> She never had so sweet a changeling;
> And jealous Oberon would have the child
> Knight of his train, to trace the forests wild....    (2.1.22–5)

This marriage, like the one celebrated by Catullus, includes in its erotic complex the additional element of homoerotic pederasty—what Oberon wants from his wife is the lovely boy. The Indian boy has no lines in the play, though he does occasionally appear in productions. In Max Reinhardt's 1935 movie, the role was played by the five-year-old Kenneth Anger in silver lamé, cute as a button, but unlikely to engage the libidinous instincts of any but the kinkiest pederast (Anger describes this as his last successful role). Lindsay Kemp's production sixty years later made the boy about twelve, knowing and seductive; Oberon had no difficulty carrying him off from the sleeping Titania and into a passionate embrace. In Santa Cruz in 1994, the director Danny Scheie moved the king and queen's libidinous investment in the boy into the world of consenting adults: he was a sulky, sexy twenty-year-old who lounged nonchalantly through the fairy scenes in nothing but a silver loincloth and some beads. The sexuality was made even more ambivalent by the fact that Oberon and Titania were chiastically cross-cast with Theseus and Hippolyta—Hippolyta played Oberon, and Theseus played Titania. Hippolyta's Oberon was suave and elegant, as thoroughly at home in the cross-dressed role as Garbo would have been. Theseus, however, was a very handsome black actor with a military bearing, who seemed distinctly uncomfortable as the fairy queen in a blonde wig and tutu. It was clear that, whichever partner this Indian boy ended up with, he would require some serious seducing. In short, in comparison with the two royal couples, Demetrius' and Lysander's quick changes of affection constitute merely the blandest kind of vanilla sexuality.

II

Magic, then, is a way of controlling sexuality and, as a corollary, of arranging marriages. The patriarchal control of sex was, indeed, an essential element in the successful maintainance of order in the family and in the state; but it is not at all clear whether magic is being presented in the play as the instrument of order, or as subversive of it. The play ends happily for everyone except Hermia's father Egeus. Egeus never agrees to his daughter's choice of a husband; and yet Egeus is acting entirely within his rights in demanding that she marry Demetrius: his daughter is legally his to dispose of. Why is the father overruled in this case? Why at least does Shakespeare not allow him a change of heart? In the folio version, he takes over the role of Philostrate as master of the wedding ceremonies, but this hardly constitutes a reconciliation. Shakespeare in revising gives him not a word of regret or good will toward the couples—half a line would have done it. The folio's Egeus merely presides over his own defeat, providing the definitive testimony to Theseus' power within the patriarchy.

One answer to his intransigence might lie in the play's darker origins. In Shakespeare's sources, Egeus is not the father of some incidental Athenian maid, but is the father of Theseus himself, the king of Athens. He commits suicide when his son, returning triumphant from the defeat of the Minotaur and the abandonment of Ariadne, neglects to change the black sails of his ship to white ones, thereby implying that he is dead. Egeus is a father destroyed by his son's carelessness. But the story is not simply an indictment of adolescent irresponsibility, because Theseus' dereliction also constitutes an assertion of power: it is his means of succeeding to his father's throne. The conflict here is the conflict of generations, and marrying Hippolyta—or Ariadne, or Phaedra—means disposing of Egeus. Prospero's magic offers a striking parallel: through it the magician is able to arrange the marriage essential to the accomplishment of his political designs; but Prospero is also very clear about the fact that the moment Ferdinand and Miranda take control of their own sexuality, he has lost them. Hence all the dire warnings against pre-marital sex; and hence the acknowledgment that, once the marriage has been celebrated, "every third thought will be [his] grave."

But magic, of course, has wider functions than the control of adolescent sex. It proposes the control of all action, the remaking of the phenomenal world according to the magician's imagination, and it therefore serves as an obvious metaphor for the playwright's art. It is not mere coincidence that at the center of *A Midsummer Night's Dream* is the production of a play, or that the identification of the archetype magician Prospero with Shakespeare has been one of the commonplaces of the critical literature. Indeed, in Shakespeare's own time, theater itself was regularly credited by its enemies with magical powers, the power to compel its audience to imitate its action; and the action is invariably conceived to be vicious, for the most part, once again, sexually. "Pride and lechery caused by players," William Rankins in 1587 warns the readers of his *Mirror of Monsters*.[4] The monsters are the actors, who have turned themselves, he says, to minotaurs—the fact that minotaurs are in the anti-theatrical discourse conceived to be dangerously, even irresistibly, attractive is surely relevant to Titania's passion for the monster Bottom. The attractiveness comes through quite clearly in Figure 4.5, Henri Fuseli's depiction of Titania's awakening, with Bottom still asleep, and not at all desexualized—there is nothing inconceivable about a love affair between these two. Similarly, for Philip Stubbes in 1583, love scenes onstage will eventuate in seduction, rape, or something unutterably worse among the spectators. "The fruits of plays and interludes" are, he says, that after theater, "everyone brings another homeward of their way very friendly, and in their secret conclaves they play the sodomites or worse."[5] Sodomy in this case does not necessarily imply homosexuality, since elsewhere in the tract Stubbes uses the term to refer to heterosexual adultery; it is simply his word for the worst kinds of sex he can imagine (he is not notably imaginative, and his rhetoric leaves room for the kinds he cannot imagine). The point is that theater provokes sex at its worst.

The classic exemplar of magical, seductive and destructive charm is the figure of Circe, and the magic of theater is compared with the charms of Circe from the very beginning of the anti-theatrical literature.[6] Unlike the invocation of minotaurs and monsters, this ominous analogy at least acknowledges the pleasurable quality of the experience. The Circean model forms yet

*Figure 4.5*    Henry Fuseli, Titania, Bottom and Oberon.
From Boydell's *Prints...Illustrating the Dramatic Works of Shakespeare*, 1803.

another subtext in *A Midsummer Night's Dream*, since the name Titania is not, in fact, a name anywhere recorded for the fairy queen. Shakespeare took it from Ovid, where it appears four times as a name for Circe, and once for Diana, thereby embodying both aspects of the power of transformation in the play, the seductive and the protective, the licentious and the chaste. If Titania is Oberon's victim, at the play's margins she is a powerful figure of both darkness and light.

The seductive and protective, indeed, comprise the nature of theater itself in the age's ethical mythology. It is not only in anti-theatrical polemics that control of the stage is assumed to confer control over the society's libido: the association of actors with licentiousness, of boy-actors and actresses with prostitution, of theaters with assignations, is a commonplace of theatrical commentary, whether in attack or defense. And yet, of course, theater was also highly regulated, and ultimately under the direct patronage of the crown, whose interests it was assumed, at least by the patrons, to serve. In fact, it may almost be said that the stage's libidinous energy was part of its point for Shakespeare's age, an element that the authorities were eager not to eliminate but to preserve. Much as the polemicists railed against the theater's bawdry, the censors looked out primarily for blasphemy and political provocation, and hardly at all for lechery. The Master of the Revels left the multitude of plots about adultery, fornication, even incest, untouched, and concerned himself instead with profane oaths, attacks on official policy, and libelous imputations against aristocrats—in short, with rebelliousness and violations of the patronage system, with God being considered the ultimate patron.

III

I return now to the figure, both enabling and disruptive, of the "fair vestal thronèd by the west." *A Midsummer Night's Dream* was produced during the long waning phase of Queen Elizabeth's reign, during which, through a combination of increasingly expensive military campaigns in the Low Countries and in Ireland, and an increasingly elaborate mythology of virginity, she undertook to reverse the tide of her growing unpopularity. The nation, beset by spiraling inflation, poor harvests, and commercial failures in major industries, looked forward to her successor, by this time generally assumed to be King James of Scotland, as eagerly as she declined to name him. To drive Catholic Spain from the Netherlands or pacify the Irish would have been a sufficient proof of her undiminished authority, but these proved elusive goals. The magic of her virginity, moreover, had only been really effective when it held out the promise of marriage, as it did for over twenty years until the failure of the negotiations over the Alençon match in 1579, the last time she was to represent herself as a marriageable woman. Her decision finally to withdraw from the marriage market was scarcely unexpected, since at the age of forty-seven it was not to be hoped that she would produce an heir. So she is thereafter figured as Astraea with her sword, the virgin goddess of Justice soon to return to heaven (Figure 4.6); or as Diana, militant chastity; or as the vestal Tuccia bearing her sieve, the emblem of her purity (Plate 13); or, more ominously, as the logical extension of the sword-bearing Astraea, a type of the fearsome biblical heroine Judith with the severed head of Holofernes, Elizabeth's chastity now offering to her male admirers not the promise of fulfillment and a throne but only what her father's marriage had offered her mother, the threat of decapitation—an image that the unfortunate Earl of Essex should probably have taken more seriously.

Nevertheless, despite the claim of inexorable virginity, the family model was still inescapable. King James initially proposed marriage to Elizabeth, but soon wooed her instead by calling her his mother. This may not have been the sort of devotion she preferred, but considering that his claim to the English throne derived from his real mother Mary Queen of Scots, the determination to switch mothers was both good politics and good manners. James's relation to Mary was, in any case, largely a political fiction, since she fled to England, and the incarceration that was to last the rest of her life, when her son was only nine months old. James is often criticized for political ineptitude, but to declare Elizabeth his mother was a stroke of genius: it transformed, with a single word, Elizabeth's chivalric romance into James's family romance, and thereby utterly changed the nature of the monarchy and the nation's expectations of it. When in 1603 the King of Scots became the King of England, there was a royal family at the center of the patriarchy for the first time since the death of Henry VIII, and there was also a patriarch.

It is no surprise, therefore (though in fact it may be mere coincidence), that *A Midsummer Night's Dream* was among the first plays chosen to be performed before the new king, on New Year's Day 1604.[7] The play was particularly appropriate to the royal interests—not only in magic and theater, but more particularly, in questions of the legal authority of fathers over their children, and the regulation and control of marriage. These were questions that had been actively debated in Parliament throughout the 1590s. In the first year of the new king's reign, the ecclesiastical authorities, in the Canons of 1604, proposed raising the age of consent from twelve to twenty-one, thereby greatly increasing paternal control over the contracting of alliances. Parliament declined to enact the necessary legislation, but the matter continued to be energetically argued. At the same time, the system of banns and marriage licenses was overhauled.

James's own interests in these matters were not merely in questions of legal jurisdiction, but in all the other powers affecting marriage and

*Figure 4.6*  Crispin van de Passe, memorial portrait of Elizabeth as Iustitia.

generation. His reasoning was significantly grounded in the world of the magical and demonic. His expertise in the subject of witchcraft is notorious; what is less often observed is that his treatise on *Daemonologie* and his attitude generally represent a significant regression from the prevailing late-Elizabethan attitudes, which were highly sceptical of the whole subject. He is not exactly gullible, in the sense that he takes a good deal of convincing; but he is certainly a believer. And witchcraft, as he discovers it, includes all the darkest implications of the magic of *A Midsummer Night's Dream*, the power not only to arrange love affairs and marriages but also to prevent them, the promise not only of erotic satisfaction but equally of sexual impotence.

James was convinced that there had been, from his youth, a systematic conspiracy against his life. Those responsible were not the political enemies that did in fact fill the early part of his reign, but witches directed by the devil. James undertook to be present at the interrogation of witches whenever possible, and their confessions, invariably extracted under torture, always confirmed his belief. English readers learned of the conspiracy, and of the king's involvement in its detection, in a pamphlet published in 1592 entitled *Newes from Scotland*. Figure 4.7 is an illustration from the pamphlet showing witches being interrogated. Three cases are described. In the first, a servant

*Figure 4.7*    The interrogation of witches, from James Carmichel,
*Newes from Scotland declaring the Damnable Life and death of Doctor Fian.*

girl named Geillis Duncane is found to possess miraculous healing powers. Though the magic seems entirely benign, her master fears her abilities are unlawful, and under torture she confesses to being a witch, and to prove the point, proceeds to perform a witches' dance for the investigators, "playing...upon a small trump."

At this point King James enters the scene:

> These confessions made the king in a wonderful admiration, and sent for the said Geillis Duncane, who upon the like trump did play the said dance before the king's majesty, who in respect of the strangeness of these matters, took great delight...[8]

—even more delight, no doubt, than he took in Oberon's dramatic magic, because Geillis Duncane is the real thing. The association of witchcraft with theater is all but explicit here.

Another case, more directly relevant to *A Midsummer Night's Dream*, concerns a schoolmaster named John Cunningham, also called Dr. Fian, under which name he was "a notable sorcerer." Cunningham took a fancy to a girl who, however, rejected his advances. He undertook to make her love him through sorcery, and persuaded her brother to "obtain for him three hairs of his sister's privities." But as the boy was attempting to fulfill his promise on the sleeping girl, she awoke. The scheme was revealed to their mother, who was a witch herself, and she substituted for her daughter's hair three hairs from the udder of a young cow. These were brought to the sorcerer, who then "wrought his art upon them," and immediately

> the cow whose hairs they were indeed came unto the door of the church wherein the schoolmaster was,...and made towards the schoolmaster, leaping and dancing upon him, and following him forth of the church and to what place soever he went, to the great admiration of all the townsmen....[9]

Figure 4.8 shows Fian, the cow, and the devil. The trope of Oberon's little western flower is domesticated, naturalized, and explicitly sexualized here— the magic of irresistible erotic attraction now lies in the female "privities." But except for the reversal of the sexes, the fantasy remains that of Oberon, Titania, and Bottom: the witch mother punishes the lascivious Fian by inventing a preposterous love affair with an animal; and the spectacle of the bestial romance provides the town with a piece of popular theater parallel-ing the courtly love of the Fairy Queen and an ass.

In the most striking of the three cases, a suspect named Agnis Tompson,[10] revealed that when James went to Denmark in 1589 to bring back his bride, the violent storms and extraordinary difficulties he experienced were caused by witchcraft. She herself had raised the storms, and was ordered by the devil

Figure 4.8    Fian and the cow, above;
Fian riding behind the devil on a black horse, below.

to kill the king by sorcery (Figure 4.9). She failed, she said, only because she could not persuade any of his faithful servants to provide her with the necessary piece of the king's soiled linen for her spells.

The king was initially sceptical of this story, and

> said they were all extreme liars, whereat she answered she would not wish his majesty to suppose her words to be false, but rather to believe them, in that she would discover such matter unto him as his majesty should not any way doubt of. And thereupon taking his majesty a little aside, she declared unto him the very words which passed between the king's majesty and his queen at Uppsala in Norway the first night of their marriage, with their answer to each other; whereat the king's majesty wondered greatly, and swore by the living God that he believed all the devils in hell could not have discovered the same, acknowledging her words to be most true....[11]

The witchcraft in this account is specifically implicated in the king's marriage. Its purpose is to forestall his return with his bride, and the crucial evidence is a revelation of the secrets of his wedding night—a proof that though Agnis Tompson failed to prevent the marriage, she nevertheless was an intimate participant in it. The story, moreover, is authenticated by the king:

Figure 4.9    The devil directs the activities of witches.
Note the sinking ship at the upper left.

like Oberon (or Henry VIII) insisting on his own cuckoldry, James is the witness to the vitiation of his marriage. James's fascination with witchcraft is obviously related to his general distrust of women, and his compulsive and public attachment to young men—the domestication, in his psychic drama, of Oberon's compulsive pursuit of the lovely Indian boy.[12] For all the romance of James's winter voyage across the North Sea to fetch his bride, he told his Privy Council that he was marrying simply to produce an heir; and he added that "as to my own nature, God is my witness, I could have abstained longer."[13] The defeat of the diabolical sorcery in fact had had nothing to do with the triumph of true love, but was rather a proof of the king's exceptional virtue: Agnis Tompson testified that "his majesty had never come safely from the sea if his faith had not prevailed above their intentions."[14] But the battle with the sorcerers would never be won: Agnis Tompson had "demanded of the devil why he did bear such hatred to the king, who answered, by reason the king is the greatest enemy he hath in the world."[15] Just as the king provides the crucial testimony to the authenticity of witchcraft, so it is the witch who validates the king's religious faith. James's queen, Anne of Denmark, it will be observed, plays no part whatever in this romantic drama.

There are obvious cultural coordinates to these fantasies. James's own career was determined by his relation to two powerful and threatening women. His mother, the libidinous—and, to Protestants, diabolical—Mary, was the source of his power, but it was a power that depended on her absence: he was king of Scotland because she was not queen. She was also his link to the English succession, but she simultaneously represented the greatest danger to his achieving it. The claim she gave him through heredity she had rendered dubious by her sexual behavior. The charge that James was illegitimate, the child of his mother's secretary David Rizzio, was widespread in the 1580s. James feared that it would weaken his chances at the English throne, and he never felt entirely free of it. He undertook to replace Mary in his family line with the chaste and regal Elizabeth, whom he was regularly addressing as his "dearest mother" by the mid-1580s. She was a mother who could give him everything he wanted—safety, wealth, legitimacy: in short, the English throne—and he courted her tirelessly; but she made no promises, ever, and would not confirm him as her heir until the moment of her death; and it is not clear that she did so even then.

Out of these crucial, unreliable, powerful, dangerous, and most important, absent women James's imagination constructed a world in which women were controlled by being incorporated. Upon his accession in 1603, he declared to Parliament that "I am the husband and the whole island is my lawful wife; I am the head, and it is my body."[16] The two statements are presented as synonymous. Mothers became unnecessary; he himself would be "a loving nourish-father" who would provide his subjects with "their own nourish-milk."[17] Psychologically, such a conception of his relation to the realm had obvious advantages. But as a political solution, James's patriarchy had a fatal weakness: it required Parliament (to whom the profligate king had constantly to turn for funds) to allow itself to be conceived as the monarch's children, or wife, or the body to his active mind, to be dictated to where it preferred to dictate, especially when it was being asked for money. Queen Elizabeth's rhetoric with the men on whom her power and purse depended had been shrewder, and much more effective: she represented them, even in her final years, as her lovers. This was, for James, in every way an impossible act to follow. When in 1609 Ben Jonson composed a *Masque of Queens* for Queen Anne and her ladies to dance in, he opened it with a coven of witches emerging from hell. Witches and queens represent the limits of the Jacobean patriarchy.

IV

Jonson's *Masque of Queens* includes a queen of the Amazons; the role was danced by his patron, Lucy Harington, Countess of Bedford. Figure 4.10 is her costume, by Inigo Jones. Jonson's Amazonian queen, however, is not Hippolyta, but Penthesilea, the Amazon who fought on the Trojan side during the Trojan War, never married, and died in combat with Achilles. Shakespeare's and Chaucer's Hippolyta, despite her impeccable poetic credentials, is for Jonson an example to be avoided, insufficiently heroic, an Amazon who preferred captivity and wedlock to a noble death; ultimately nothing in herself, but only a trophy of Theseus' triumph, or even less, a mere token of the bond between Hercules and his martial companion.

Oberon, however, figures significantly in Jonson's creation of a Jacobean royal mythology. Two years after *The Masque of Queens*, Jonson and Jones produced the masque of *Oberon*, the title character being now not the king but the crown prince of fairyland, with the role danced by the sixteen-year-old Henry Prince of Wales, shown in Figure 4.11 in the costume Jones designed for him. As a court masque, *Oberon* includes a good deal of the celebratory tone of *A Midsummer Night's Dream*, and even some of its eroticism. It opens, like Shakespeare's play, in moonlight, with a group of satyrs awaiting the appearance of the fairy prince. The mildly priapic dancers in Figure 4.12 have always been identified with this scene, but given their stylistic incompatibility with the other drawings for *Oberon*, they are unlikely to be designs for this masque, and given their indecency they are unlikely to be related to any performance at court. (I include them simply because they show Jones imagining satyrs.) They amuse themselves by anatomizing their pastimes, which are the courtly pleasures of dancing, drinking, and making love. Jonson's mythology, like Shakespeare's, is an unabashed mixture of classical and native. The satyrs, and their leader Silenus, are solidly grounded in ancient sources that Jonson cites in copious marginal notes. The fairies of Oberon's court, on the other hand, are recognizably English, emanations, in the costume designs, of Inigo Jones's idealized medievalism (Figure 4.13). No sources are cited for Oberon himself, partly because the figure derives from the more ephemeral traditions of folktale and popular theater, but more significantly because Jonson's Oberon in fact has his source primarily in the world of Jacobean politics and the royal family drama.

Jonson and Jones present Oberon as a romantic hero; and unlike the fairies he rules, he is firmly classicized in a costume derived from Roman imperial armor. But if Oberon is the fairy prince, who in this fable is the king? Queen Elizabeth had been central to the magic of *A Midsummer Night's Dream*, a principle necessary to the plot, the element that explains everything. She remains, nevertheless, marginal to the action—she is only a principle of explanation. But King James is in every way the center of *Oberon*; in this masque designed to celebrate the creation of the king's elder son as Prince of Wales, Jonson's focus is firmly on the royal throne, the hereditary chair of King Arthur. James

Figure 4.10   Inigo Jones, costume for Lucy,
Countess of Bedford as Penthesilea in *The Masque of Queens*, 1609.

*Figure 4.11*   Inigo Jones, costume for Henry,
Prince of Wales, in the title role in *Oberon*, 1611.

*Figure 4.12*    Inigo Jones, dancing satyrs, probably not related to *Oberon*.

sits on a raised dais at the center of the audience, at the focal point of the
scenic perspective, the only perfect place from which to view Inigo Jones's
scenic machine; the spectacle is his. Oberon, therefore, is as much spectator
as spectacle; his musicians do not sing his praise, but rather

> ...in tunes to Arthur's chair
> Bear Oberon's desire,
> Than which there nothing can be higher,
> Save James, to whom it flies:    (222–5)

Figure 4.13    Inigo Jones, fairies in *Oberon*.

Oberon's desire flies outward and upward, to his royal father—the masque is not, after all, a celebration of the prince, but a celebration offered by Oberon and his knights to James's glory,

> To whose sole power and magic they do give
> The honor of their being....    (249–50)

So much, in the world of court politics and patronage, is no more than the literal truth. But of course Oberon's desire for Arthur's throne is not simply an act of homage to his father. Jonson's rhetoric itself betrays the anxieties inherent on both sides in the naming of a successor. Behind Oberon's public filial homage lies a complex family drama. James and Prince Henry were in fact by 1611 political opponents, James a programmatic pacifist eager for accommodations with the Catholic powers on the continent, Henry a militant Protestant, eager to lead an army of liberation through Germany and the Low Countries. By the age of fourteen, the prince's military ambitions were being noted with enthusiasm throughout the country, and by the time he was formally declared James's heir, his popular following made him a serious rival to the king in matters of public and foreign policy. Figure 4.14 shows him as he was represented in a popular engraving. The heroic persona devised by Jonson and Jones for the prince in *Oberon* thus expressed not only ideals but intentions, and chivalric imagery here had

Figure 4.14    William Hole, Prince Henry at the Lance,
dedicatory engraving from Michael Drayton's *Poly-Olbion*, 1613.

nothing to do with courtly love and social graces, and everything to do with military exercises and ultimately with the training of armies. *Oberon* was, in its way, a declaration of war, and King James did his best to counteract it. The prince had wanted his masque to culminate with martial games in which he could distinguish himself. But the king insisted that *Oberon* conclude instead with the dances and songs of courtly society. The prince was disarmed, even as he was idealized.

James's rivalry with Prince Henry crystallized at this time around the issue of his marriage. The king was determined on Catholic matches for both the Crown Prince and his sister Elizabeth, marriages of state that would form part of the larger plan for a rapprochement with Catholic Spain and France. As in the case of Egeus and Hermia, James's children's hands were entirely within his gift; and though Henry opposed a marriage to any but a Protestant, it was nevertheless perfectly clear to him what was involved and where his duty lay. He was obliged to assure his father in writing that it was "for your majesty to resolve what course is most convenient to be taken by the rules of state."[18]

To marry Prince Henry to a Catholic princess was also effectively to disarm him as a Protestant hero—this was, at any rate, the most James could do to ensure that his pacifism would extend into the next generation. But all the negotiations fell through, and in 1612 James yielded so far as to allow Princess Elizabeth to be betrothed to the Protestant suitor strongly favored by Prince Henry, Frederick, the Elector Palatine, subsequently—briefly—king of Bohemia. Henry's intention was to follow his sister and brother-in-law to the continent at the head of a Protestant army, something the Prince of Wales would certainly not have been permitted to do. It was only his sudden death in 1612, of typhoid fever, that prevented the heroic role of Oberon from being translated into a drama of open hostility between father and son. Queen Anne, and a significant segment of the British public, always believed that the prince had been poisoned; even the king was not beyond suspicion. He was, after all, the logical suspect: it was he who profited most from Prince Henry's death.

The rivalry of the generations returns us, finally, to those happy marriages at the end of *A Midsummer Night's Dream*, that comedy poised on the edge of tragedy, the comedy that just precedes *Phaedra*, *The Winter's Tale*, the family drama of the Jacobean crown. When Bottom awakes from his vision of love and transfiguration he says he will call it Bottom's Dream, not because it is his, but "because it hath no bottom"—because, as we would say, you can't get to the bottom of it. No account, no explanation, can exhaust the implications of patriarchal ideology; it keeps returning, if not as *Romeo and Juliet* then as *Pyramus and Thisbe*: the subject can be parodied, but never exorcised. In this culture's version of the Oedipus story, Laius always wins.

# FIVE

## The Pornographic Ideal

I turn now from the interrelations of text, performance, interpretation and history in a particular play to a much narrower example: a Shakespearean text of only two words that has become a notorious crux for both performers and editors. Near the end of *The Winter's Tale* we are told of a sur-passingly lifelike statue of the late queen Hermione, the work of "that rare Italian master Giulio Romano," commissioned and owned by the noble Paulina, connoisseur and architect of the play's reconciliations. In the final scene, the statue is revealed, and brought to life. The invocation of Giulio Romano is striking for a number of reasons: this is the only allusion in Shakespeare to a modern artist and, indeed, one of the earliest references to Giulio in England—Shakespeare here, as nowhere else, appears to be in touch with the avant-garde of the visual arts. But Giulio was not a sculptor, and in fact the name is all the play gives us. As it turns out, there is no statue; the figure Paulina unveils is the living queen. What is in that name; how are we to understand this most minimal of texts and—the ultimate question for a play—how are we to perform it?

I begin, however, not with Shakespeare but with the most famous—or notorious—of Giulio Romano's works, a set of unspeakable, and soon invisible, images, obscene in the original sense: representing what may not be brought on stage, may not be represented. They were suppressed by papal order and almost entirely obliterated in their own time, but nevertheless survived through the survival of their accompanying texts, their explana-tions. The images are the scandalous suite of sexual positions known as I Modi, engraved from Giulio's drawings by Marcantonio Raimondi in 1524; the texts are Pietro Aretino's sonnets, written in the following year to be published with them. For almost four centuries these works have been a touchstone for the pornographic ideal—Vasari, indeed, refers to them as "the loves of the gods"—their perfection only underlined by the fact of their disappearance.

112

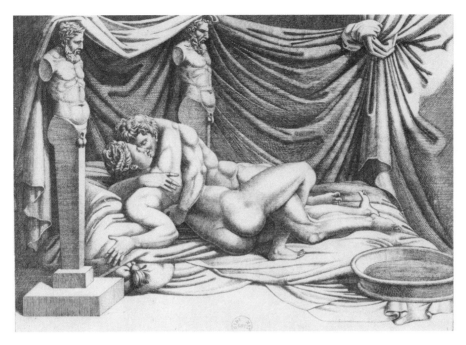

Figure 5.1    Marcantonio Raimondi, engraving after Giulio Romano, *I Modi*, first position.

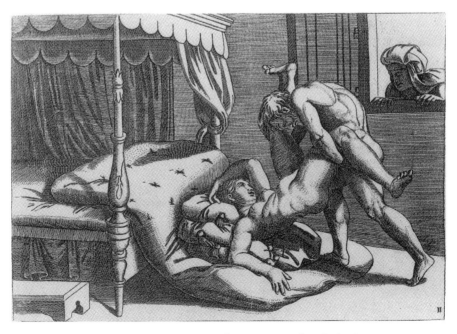

Figure 5.2    Marcantonio Raimondi, engraving after Giulio Romano,
*I Modi*, eleventh position.

Figure 5.3    *I Modi*, woodcut 1.

As it turns out, however, they did not quite disappear. Two prints from the original series survive. The first of the *Modi*, Figure 5.1, is not the missionary position, to be sure, but also seems nothing for Pope Julius to get excited about. The other surviving print, Figure 5.2, the eleventh of the sixteen, is more athletic, and includes the exciting presence of a voyeur. But there also survives a unique exemplar of a volume of woodcut copies of the whole suite, along with the sonnets, probably published in 1527 in Venice.[1] The woodcuts are a good deal cruder than the engravings, but Aretino's text is richly expressive. In Figure 5.3, corresponding to the first Marcantonio print, it is not even clear what kind of sex is in progress. Aretino, however, clarifies the action, if not the position: "Let's fuck, my love, let's fuck quickly," etc. (I have avoided any coyness in translating the Italian terms *fottere*, *potta*, *cazzo*, etc.: the sonnets are both crude and entirely explicit.) The action is all quite straightforward, with the only offbeat moment provided by the man's final plea that the woman take his testicles inside her along with his penis. The second position, in Figure 5.4, looks equally straightforward (or at least as if it will end up being so); but for Aretino it starts to get kinky: "*Mettimi un dito in cul*," "Stick your finger in my ass," the woman urges, and later tells her lover that if he is bored with her vagina he is welcome to her anus, concluding that "*uomo non è chi non è bugerone*"—"A man isn't a man unless he's a bugger," or perhaps more simply, "There isn't a man who isn't a bugger." The lover reassures her; he is a man, he wants both. There is nothing in the print to suggest this line of pillow talk, though of course Aretino may have got his information about what was really going on from Giulio himself, and in that case the image would be dependent in the most literal sense on the presence of the word.

If Aretino is correct about what is really happening in this print, then buggery is present in the erotic progress of the series almost from the beginning. Indeed, as one proceeds through the volume, the intensity of its interest in buggery becomes increasingly noticeable—in almost every sonnet,

Figure 5.4    I Modi, woodcut 2.

women want it as much as men want to do it. Some of this may, of course, represent Aretino's interests more than Giulio's, though as Figures 5.5 and 5.6, the tenth and sixteenth of the positions, indicate, there is plenty of explicit sodomy in the prints; and it is therefore worth remarking that the couples are throughout heterosexual—there is no equivalent to Giulio's recognition when he depicted the Orpheus story, for example, that men do sometimes ignore women in favor of other men, and that the anus, in any case, is not gendered.[2] But in fact, though every orifice that is represented as penetrated is female, for the viewer (or voyeur) the visual temptations strongly solicit homoerotic tastes as well. Consider, for example, the third print, Figure 5.7. "*Questo cazzo voglio*," the sonnet opens with the woman speaking, but the print displays an impressive pair of male buttocks at work—this is what the viewer is assumed to want. An even more striking example is the ninth print, Figure 5.8: here the man is exciting himself by looking at the woman's buttocks, perhaps with a suggestion that he is going to beat her. Aretino has him explain that he has to take his pleasure this way because of his "*poco cazzo*," little prick—

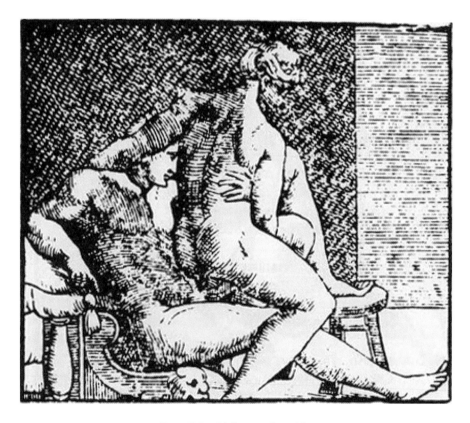

*Figure 5.5    Modi, woodcut 10.*

Figure 5.6    Modi, woodcut 16.

as the third sonnet advises, "Chi n'ha poco in cul fotta," "Men who don't have much should fuck the ass." But the tempting, open buttocks presented to our view are not hers but his—and the viewer of these prints is certainly assumed to be male. Giulio is clearly catering to well defined tastes; for comparison, Figure 5.9 is the view of Apollo in his chariot that he provided for his Gonzaga patrons in the heavens of the Palazzo Tè.

In fact, though the enjoyment is represented as entirely mutual, there is a good deal more in I Modi for men than for women. The men range from youthful Adonises to elderly lechers, but the women are all young, firm, rounded: there is, in Giulio's libidinous world, a beautiful woman eager to satisfy any man of whatever age or appearance. For the woman who is less than glamorous, however, there is nothing but voyeurism. At the same time, although these fantasies are predicated on the notion that men can have absolutely anything they want in the way of sex, the range of imagined erotic possibilities is remarkably limited. Men enjoy themselves and satisfy their

*Figure 5.7    I Modi, woodcut 3.*

women by plugging either of their holes in a variety of increasingly athletic positions. In addition, homosexual sodomy is suggested, if only by implication—perhaps Giulio always sensed the threat of the vengeful maenads pursuing Orpheus after he turned to the love of boys. But the sex stops there. There are no other erogenous zones; not even women's breasts are represented as erotically interesting, and oral sex of any sort, including kissing, is quite outside the repertory. The attention of both men and women is totally focused on the *cazzo*, the *potta*, the *culo*. Indeed, the most sexually daring element of the figures in I *Modi* is certainly what is provided for them by Aretino's sonnets, their ability to talk dirty.

By the end of the century the sonnets had in effect become the pictures, in part because they constituted the only way of realizing Giulio's famous, now suppressed images. Thus Agostino Carraci's pornographic collection of loves of the gods is called *L'Aretino.* But there is a recognition as well of how deeply

*Figure 5.8   I Modi*, woodcut 9.

the images depend on their texts: Ben Jonson's Lady Politic Would-be, showing off her knowledge of Italian culture to Volpone, enthusiastically cites, "for a desperate wit...Aretine/ Only his pictures are a little obscene" (3.4.96); and Corvino uses, as the model of the lecherous imagination, "some young Frenchman, or hot Tuscan blood/ That had read Aretine, conned all his prints" (3.7.59–60). Jonson knew about Giulio Romano, citing him twice in lists of pre-eminent modern artists, but as the creator of the *Modi* he has disappeared, to be replaced by his librettist. Indeed, the English were being explicitly taught to read Aretino: John Florio's sources for *Queen Anna's New World of Words* (1611), the great Italian-English dictionary, include—along with the canonical Petrarch, Boccaccio, Castiglione, Tasso, Machiavelli—the vocabulary of Aretino as well; and Florio witholds nothing. Under *potta* Queen Anne would have found "a woman's cunt," under *pottaccia*, "a filthy great cunt."

It is generally agreed that Shakespeare's choice of Giulio Romano as the sculptor for the nonexistent statue of the supposedly dead Hermione that Paulina pretends to resuscitate at the conclusion of *The Winter's Tale* is unlikely to have been dictated by the experience of any actual work of art. Certainly Shakespeare did not see any Giulio Romano sculptures, because there are

*Figure 5.9*    Giulio Romano, Apollo in his Chariot.
Ceiling fresco in the Palazzo Tè, Mantua.

none. I have very little to add to the arguments about how Giulio in particular gets into the play (for a fuller discussion of the matter see the introduction to my Oxford edition of *The Winter's Tale*), but it does seem to me significant that a named, modern artist is invoked, rather than an invented one, or a historical figure like Phidias or Zeuxis, who might reasonably be represented as providing art works to collectors in ancient Sicily. The artist's name, the briefest of texts, is everything, and in this context, in 1610, it is Aretino who is being suppressed.

Paulina is presented in the play as a connoisseur, the owner of a superlative art collection, and her expertise reminds us that the collecting instinct was starting to burgeon in the England of 1610—there is, indeed, a formidable contemporary model for Paulina in the Countess of Arundel. She and the Earl formed the greatest collection of art works in Jacobean England. They owned a number of Giulio's drawings, including preparatory sketches for the luxuriantly erotic frescos at the Palazzo Tè, though these had not been acquired by 1610, and the Arundels' interests were certainly in Giulio as a history painter rather than as a pornographer. But the Arundel circle would have been a good source of information as to which artists were especially adept at producing the lifelike.

There was, in fact, a good deal of information circulating in Shakespeare's England about who were the right artists to invest in. Richard Haydocke in 1598 noted "many noblemen then furnishing their houses with the excellent monuments of sundry famous and ancient masters, both Italian and German,"[3] and English collectors in the first decade of the seventeenth century began for the first time to be serious connoisseurs, dispatching experts to the continent to buy for them, and concerned with acquiring expertise of their own. In 1609, the Earl of Exeter was advising the Earl of Shrewsbury to purchase paintings by Palma Giovane and sculpture by Giambologna;[4] and Prince Henry became a passionate collector of paintings and bronzes. By 1610 Inigo Jones was contributing his expert eye and artistic authority to the refinement of aristocratic English taste: he had traveled in Italy observing and sketching, and advised first the Earl of Rutland on artistic matters, and later Prince Henry.

In Europe for more than a century great art collections had been a conspicuous attribute of aristocratic magnificence. Henry VIII, like his contemporaries Francis I and Charles V, invested heavily in painting, sculpture and tapestries, and though there were no Titians in the Tudor royal gallery, the Holbeins and Torrigianos imply a very high standard of artistic taste. Taste, however, was an extravagance that the English monarchy could subsequently ill afford. Edward and Mary had other matters to occupy them, and neither Elizabeth nor James had much interest in the arts as such, and none whatever in increasing the royal picture gallery. Prince Charles, however, shared his brother's artistic passion, and inherited most of his treasures on Prince Henry's death in 1612. Thereafter he collected voraciously. By the mid-1630s the Caroline royal pictures constituted one of the greatest art collections in the world. Increasingly in this period great art was felt, in a way that was at once pragmatic and mystical, to be a manifestation of the power and authority of its possessor. Great artists became essential to the developing concept of monarchy and to the idealization of the aristocracy, to realize and deploy the imagery of legitimacy and greatness.

The art is important, then, and the choice of the artist is critical. Why Giulio Romano? The answer, such as it is, is usually found in an epitaph for Giulio quoted in Vasari, beginning "*Videbat Jupiter corpora sculpta pictaque…*": "Jupiter saw sculpted and painted bodies breathe and the houses of mortals made equal to those in heaven through the skill of Giulio Romano." Giulio was, then, known in the sixteenth century as a sculptor—or at least anyone reading Vasari would think he was. I am not the first to point out that *sculpta* can also mean "engraved," and that the reference may, therefore, be to the myriad of prints produced from Giulio's work, including the famous, obscene, suppressed, and by Shakespeare's time all but nonexistent prints of I *Modi*. But it is also worth remarking on the fact that in a period when connoisseurship was rapidly developing and actively pursued, Shakespeare, or whoever was advising him, should have gone not to a gallery or to the art market to find his paragon (say Michelangelo, Cellini, or Giambologna), but to the text that constitutes the beginning of art history.[5]

If it was indeed Vasari's *Lives* that led Shakespeare, however indirectly, to Giulio, the artist's biography offered the playwright a curiously appropriate touchstone for The Winter's Tale. For Vasari, Giulio's crucial quality is not only his illusionistic talent, but the ability to represent the human as divine, particularly through sexuality. Here is Shakespeare's Florizel wooing Perdita:

> Apprehend
> Nothing but jollity. The gods themselves,
> Humbling their deities to love, have taken
> The shapes of beasts upon them. Jupiter
> Became a bull, and bellowed; the green Neptune
> A ram, and bleated; and the fire-robed god,
> Golden Apollo, a poor humble swain,
> As I seem now.   (4.4.24–31)

Florizel goes on to assure Perdita that his intentions are entirely pure and chaste, but his choice of divine role-models places him firmly in an Ovidian world where lust is the divine principle and rape the essential creative act. Vasari, in the same way, believed that the *Modi* represented not simply sex in action, but divine sex, specifically the loves of the gods—which probably indicates that he had not only never seen the prints, but had never read the Aretino sonnets either. Still, Vasari is not entirely misguided, in that the ability to render sexuality both explicit and ideal is certainly one of Giulio's most obvious talents: Jove and Olimpia, on a wall of the Palazzo Tè (Plate 14), testify to the fact that a project like I Modi was only awaiting the right patron, and Cupid and Psyche, on the opposite wall preparing for their wedding night (Figure 5.10), are both equally desirable, appearing ready not only for each other, but for anyone else. In a post-coital scene (Plate 15), the viewer seems to be offered everything that Aretino's scurrilous commentaries promise: a graceful, compliant, sexually active Cupid, and Psyche's rear end.

We are not used to thinking of Shakespeare's drama in this way, but it really does belong to the same sexual world. Mercutio taunts Romeo:

> Now will he sit under a medlar tree
> And wish his mistress were that kind of fruit
> As maids call medlars when they lie alone....

The medlar is slang for the vagina. Mercutio continues,

> O Romeo, that she were, O that she were
> An open-arse, thou a pop'rin pear!

"Open-arse" is the popular name for the medlar, and a poperin or popering pear is an ordinary pear, the familiar phallic-shaped fruit. The identification of vaginas with open arses assumes that only women are penetrable, but the very openness of the vulgar epithet belies the assumption. Similarly, at the end of The Merchant of Venice, Gratiano has a polymorphous fantasy that has gone almost unnoticed by critics and commentators. He has been given a ring as a love token by his fiancée Nerissa, which he has been persuaded to give up, in gratitude for the rescue of Antonio from the danger of Shylock's knife; he has given it to a young lawyer's clerk, who is, of course, Nerissa in disguise. After all the accusations and explanations are over, and the lovers are finally reconciled, Gratiano conceives of his wedding night in terms of being in bed with the young man to whom he gave Nerissa's ring:

> ...were the day come, I should wish it dark
> Till I were couching with the doctor's clerk.
> Well, while I live I'll fear no other thing
> So sore as keeping safe Nerissa's ring—

"ring" being not simply the love token, but a word for both the vagina and the anus (of which "ring" is a literal translation): the front, the rear, male,

*Figure 5.10*    Giulio Romano, Cupid and Psyche bathing. Fresco in the Palazzo Tè, Mantua.

female—even sexually, Nerissa and the doctor's clerk are equivalents and alternatives.

The imagined world of sexuality in *The Winter's Tale*, too, is the world of Giulio Romano, both in its idealized Ovidian incarnation and its Aretine naturalism; these are inseparable complements in the play, just as the subtext of Giulio's idealized *Marriage of Cupid and Psyche* is the uncontrollable libido of *I Modi*. The gods for Florizel are sexual animals; Perdita masquerades as Flora and invokes Proserpina, both victims of divine rape. All women in Leontes' imagination are bawds, "as false as o'er-dyed blacks, as winds, as waters," insatiable and indiscriminate, willing to "let in and out the enemy / With bag and baggage"; while men are unable to resist their seductive availability, even at the cost of friendship or a crown. Leontes, indeed, proves the point in himself, lusting even after the restored Perdita, young enough to be his daughter—which in fact she is—when she reappears at his court as Florizel's fiancée. Sexuality is a constant; it is the art of Giulio Romano, the miraculous living statue, that enables the play to find in the animal lust of Leontes' (or, for that matter, Florizel's) imagination a love worthy of the gods.

But of course there is no statue, and never was one. The statue exists only in Paulina's charade; even the charade is absent from Robert Greene's novel *Pandosto*, Shakespeare's source for the plot of the play, in which the queen simply dies and remains dead; and, as we have seen, the statue scarcely, at most ambiguously, exists even as a possibility in Vasari—if that was Shakespeare's source for the name of Giulio Romano. The statue, like the artist's name, is a figment, a fiction, a text, a discourse, ultimately a performance, whose sole function is to relieve the king of his guilt and restore his losses. It has been the impossible task of four hundred years of stage history to realize that text, and produce out of the mere name Giulio Romano a credible work of art. Four hundred years of pornography had, in Aretino's sonnets, a good deal more to work with. I turn now to the metamorphoses of the statue.

For audiences and critics since the early nineteenth century, the statue scene has been both emotionally central and dramatically essential, a triumph of love and patience with mystical overtones that constitutes the tragicomic resolution. It has also epitomized the play's profound ambivalence, an utterly implausible device that is nevertheless theatrically foolproof, and over the past three centuries has earned as much scorn as praise for its blatant theatricality. Even for hostile critics, however, the play has been difficult to imagine without it; and indeed, it is quintessentially Shakespearean in the sense that Shakespeare added it to the plot he found in Greene: the statue is all Shakespeare. How far it epitomizes the Shakespeare of Jacobean audiences, however, is another question. The only surviving account of the play in its own time (which is the only account of any performance before the mid-eighteenth century) makes no mention of Hermione's statue coming to life. The physician and astrologer Simon Forman saw *The Winter's Tale* at the Globe in 1611, when it was new, and recorded a summary of its action in his diary. Here is the account, in a modernized text:

> In *The Winter's Tale* at the Globe 1611 the 15 of May Wednesday, observe there how Leontes the King of Sicilia was overcome with jealousy of his wife with the King of Bohemia, his friend that came to see him, and how he contrived his death and would have had his cupbearer to have poisoned, who gave the King of Bohemia warning thereof and fled with him to Bohemia.
>
> Remember also how he sent to the oracle of Apollo, and the answer of Apollo, that she was guiltless and that the King was jealous, etc., and how except the child was found again that was lost the King should die without issue, for the child was carried into Bohemia and there laid in a forest and brought up by a shepherd. And the King of Bohemia his son married that wench, and how they fled into Sicilia to Leontes, and the shepherd having showed the letter of the nobleman by whom Leontes sent away that child, and the jewels found about her, she was known to be Leontes' daughter, and was then sixteen years old.
>
> Remember also the rogue that came in all tattered like colt-pixie,[6] and how he feigned him sick and to have been robbed of all that he had, and how he cozened the poor man of all his money, and after came to the sheep-shear with a pedlar's pack and there cozened them again of all their money, and how he changed apparel with the King of Bohemia his son, and then how he turned courtier, etc. Beware of trusting feigned beggars or fawning fellows.

The statue is not all that is missing from this version of *The Winter's Tale*. Forman has little interest in Hermione and none whatever in Paulina, the deaths of Mamillius and Antigonus, or the notorious bear; his focus is on the kings, the jealousy, the plotting, the money, finally on the rogue Autolycus. Redemption in Forman's *Winter's Tale* comes not through the miracle of forgiveness and reconciliation, but through the restoration of Perdita. Even so, the moral he takes away from his afternoon at the Globe and inscribes among his notes for "common policy" (i.e., the conduct of everyday affairs) has nothing to do with family feeling, dynastic imperatives or the dangers of paranoid jealousy, but something much more commonplace: "beware of trusting feigned beggars or fawning fellows."

Forman's omission of the statue scene has been used to argue that the miraculous conclusion is a revision, and that the play originally followed its source in leaving the queen dead. But Forman is too unreliable a reporter to be used in this way: his accounts of both *Macbeth* and *Cymbeline*, which he saw in the same season, also diverge significantly from the texts. The most we can conclude from Forman's evidence (it is in fact a good deal) is that what at least one Jacobean spectator carried home from the original *Winter's Tale* did not include a scene that no audience or reader since the eighteenth century has been able to ignore. But however eccentric a witness Forman may be, he is not at all eccentric in one respect: although twenty allusions to the play survive from the seventeenth century (about as many as for *King Lear* and *Henry V*, almost double the number for *As You Like It*), not one of these refers to the statue or the return of Hermione. Our surviving witnesses were for the most part interested, as Simon Forman was, in Autolycus. Outside the text of the four Shakespeare folios, there is no reference whatever to the statue scene remaining from the seventeenth century.

From the time the play reappeared in the eighteenth century, however, the statue scene increasingly became its emotional center. Nicholas Rowe's Shakespeare, the first illustrated edition, published in 1709, chose the statue scene for the play's frontispiece (Figure 5.11). This realization cannot be derived from stage practice, since the play had not been performed since at least 1640, but despite the fact that the scene had apparently disappeared from the collective memory of the play, for producers and artists the statue was of the essence in conceptualizing the drama. The costumes are a curious mixture of Roman for the men and largely contemporary for the women (Polixenes, just behind Leontes, is in a variety of exotic dress, intended as Bohemian), but what is most striking about the scene is the absolute dominance of Hermione, her scepter raised in a gesture of command. In the text, the scene is firmly under the direction of Paulina, who stage-manages the restoration and reconciliation, but all the women here express surprise. The figure immediately to the left of Hermione is presumably intended as Paulina, but her gesture is identical to that of the amazed Leontes, and she is distinctly subordinate to the queen.

Indeed, the artist's imagination gives the moment of Hermione's revival a dramatic authority that it was not to have again in the theatre for almost a century.

The scene was so popular that it was often played by itself, as a prelude or coda to another play, a miniature sentimental melodrama guaranteeing a receptive and responsive audience for the main event of the evening. I have given a detailed account of the transformations of the statue scene in my Oxford edition of *The Winter's Tale*. I focus here, therefore, on a small number of theatrical landmarks. It was another half century before the play at last returned to the stage. Mrs Pritchard's commanding Hermione, in Figure 5.12, wears classical drapery that suggests a shroud, but she also wears a large pendent cross—this is in Garrick's version of the play, which concentrates on the pastoral sections, and was therefore renamed *Florizel and Perdita*. It omits the first three acts, and with them most of the classical context.

Figure 5.11  Frontispiece to *The Winter's Tale* from Nicholas Rowe's Shakespeare, 1709.

*Figure 5.12*    Hannah Pritchard as Hermione in Garrick's *Florizel and Perdita*.
Engraving after a lost painting by R. E. Pine, *c.* 1760.

Nothing in Garrick's text, therefore, contradicted this visual assertion of the
queen's Christian faith.

A generation later, Elizabeth Farren's Hermione (Figure 5.13), also in
Garrick's version, is notably more stylish, and much younger. The iconography here is classical: a bas relief on her pedestal shows putti performing two
scenes from Euripides' *Alcestis*, Herakles leading the queen back from the
dead, and the reuniting of Alcestis and Admetus. In contrast, Elizabeth Hartley
(Figure 5.14), in 1780 in Drury Lane, is fashionably contemporary, posed in
an elegant neoclassical niche, wearing an informal evening gown (court dress
would have called for a hoopskirt) and an elaborate coiffure.

*Figure 5.13* Elizabeth Farren as Hermione, *c. 1780.*
Engraving after a painting by Johann Zoffany.

*Figure 5.14* Elizabeth Hartley as Hermione, c. 1780.

In all these versions, the play consisted only of its pastoral scenes and the concluding reconciliation. The play's first three acts—Leontes' jealousy, the deaths of Hermione and Mamillius, the abandonment of Perdita and the death of Antigonus with the famous bear in pursuit—were only finally restored in John Philip Kemble's *Winter's Tale*, first produced in 1802. Returning the play to Shakespeare, however, meant restoring the play's anachronisms. Initially, these were not a major issue. Productions such as Kemble's, and Macready's in 1837, moved unproblematically between Sicily and Bohemia, ancient and recent. But by the middle of the century, the historicising imagination had taken control even of this most temporally vagrant of scripts. In 1856, Charles Kean presented a spectacular and thoroughly archeologized version of the play. Leontes' Sicily was arbitrarily but firmly placed in the fourth century B.C. (Figure 5.15 shows the set for Leontes' palace), and all anachronisms were excised: there were therefore no references to the emperor of Russia, Whitsun pastorals, saint-like sorrows, Judas Iscariot—or Giulio Romano. Historically authentic fourth-century costumes and properties were employed; these were derived from the palpable evidence of vase paintings and ancient artefacts: Shakespeare's fairy tale became a re-creation of the ancient world, historically rationalized. To deal with the fact that Bohemia not only has no seacoast but did not even exist in the fourth century, the

Figure 5.15    I. Dayes, setting for the opening scene
of Charles Kean's production of *The Winter's Tale*, 1856.

country was emended to Bithynia—the emendation had been proposed by Hanmer a century earlier, but found no favor with editors. Figure 5.16 is the artist's design for the statue scene. Hermione, played by Ellen Tree—Mrs Charles Kean—stands in a columned shrine, a slim figure classically draped; Leontes, Perdita, Polixenes and Paulina are in deep shadow, surrounded by a multitude of witnesses.

Figure 5.16    I. Dayes, design for the statue scene in Kean's *Winter's Tale*, 1856.

C. R. Leslie's portrait of Mrs Kean's Hermione (Figure 5.17) shows her as sleek, graceful and majestic, every inch a queen. Ellen Terry, however, paints a different picture, one where Kean's archeology was defeated by his queen's sense of herself—and where ancient history was defeated by modern propriety. Terry made her debut playing Mamillius in this production at the age of nine (Figure 5.18). In her memoirs she recalls that, whatever the role, Mrs Kean always wore her hair in the same modern fashion, parted in the middle and pulled tight around her head. And, she continues—quite contradicting the slim, graceful figure in Leslie's portrait—"the amount of petticoats she wore. Even as Hermione she was always bunched out by layer upon layer of petticoats," utterly destroying the classical effect.

Alas for the camera! Figure 5.19 is a photograph of Mrs Kean as Hermione: for all her drapery, she is immediately identifiable as a Victorian matron,

Figure 5.17    C. R. Leslie, Mrs Charles Kean as Hermione in *The Winter's Tale*.

*Figure* 5.18    Ellen Terry as Mamillius and Charles Kean as Leontes, 1856.

*Figure 5.19*  Ellen Tree (Mrs Charles Kean) as Hermione, 1856.

*Figure 5.20*    Ellen Terry as Hermione, His Majesty's Theatre, 1906.

Figure 5.21    Mary Anderson as Hermione, Lyceum, 1887.

much more insistently of her period than the equally individualized and
unidealized Hermione of Mrs Pritchard a century earlier. To modern eyes, it
is difficult to accommodate this unglamorous, definitively middle-aged figure
to the romance of reconciliations and restored losses at the play's
conclusion—the camera reveals that C. R. Leslie's artistic eye was an editorial
one as well.[7] But this in a sense is our problem: the image is true to the play
in a way that over the centuries, few interpreters, theatrical or critical, have
been willing to be. Mrs Kean's Hermione takes seriously the losses and the
passage of time—as, in fact, Kean's text did not: Leontes' observation that
"Hermione was not so much wrinkled, nothing/ So agèd as this seems"
(5.3.28–9) was cut, as it regularly was from eighteenth- and nineteenth-

*Figure* 5.22    Mary Anderson as Perdita, Lyceum, 1887.

century performing texts, until Beerbohm Tree restored it in 1906, with Ellen Terry, in Figure 5.20, having outgrown Mamillius to become, at the age of fifty-nine, the most agelessly beautiful of Hermiones.

The denial of the realities of time in the play reached a logical apogee when the American actress Mary Anderson, in 1887, for the first time doubled as both Hermione and her daughter Perdita. Figure 5.21 shows her as Hermione, Figure 5.22 as Perdita, at which she looks rather less convincing (she was only twenty-eight at the time, so she probably did bring it off). The costumes, correctly classical, were by Alma-Tadema, and the production strove above all to be pre-eminently tasteful. To this end the play was heavily cut; Anderson explained that Shakespearean texts were a mixture of authentic beauties adulterated with actors' and printers' interpolations, and she undertook to reduce the play to the authentically Shakespearean, which she took to be the tasteful. Therefore references to sexuality, and to the darker passions generally, including all Leontes' soliloquies on his jealousy, were omitted, as were even references to Hermione's pregnancy and Paulina's recriminations after Hermione's death—in short, most of the drama of the first half of the play was considered tasteless and was cut. The performing time was reduced to a little over two hours, and the success of the production was immense and unqualified: it lasted 164 nights, and was the longest-running production of *The Winter's Tale* in England or America in the nineteenth century.

The doubling of Hermione and Perdita is more a tour de force for the actress than a viable option for the play, but its theatrical value—and it is difficult to see it as anything but a sentimentalizing device—has been felt by many actresses and directors since 1887. In Mary Anderson's case, it necessitated depriving Perdita of her lines in the last scene: to restore the mother meant silencing the daughter, and reviewers were generally unconvinced. When Judi Dench doubled Hermione and Perdita at Stratford in 1969, Trevor Nunn devised an ingenious way of allowing Hermione to perform a quick change into Perdita, thus enabling the daughter to retain her lines; but once again, many viewers found the device unpersuasive—when I saw the production, I found myself unable to concentrate on anything except how the trick was to be done. And yet the idea of doubling the roles remains attractive, if only as an antidote to the hardest truths of the play. It renders nugatory, for example, Leontes' moment of lust for the unrecognized Perdita (and consequently, this was one of the few bits of sexual innuendo that Mary Anderson's production felt safe in retaining): if Leontes making a move on his daughter is merely affirming his unaltered love for his wife, the dangers of incest and the tension between the generations need not be considered, and in the passage of sixteen years, nothing at all has been lost.

In 1912, Granville Barker returned the full text of the play to the stage in a genuinely innovative production. Eschewing any pretence to the historical, it was set on a thrust stage with sets recalling both modernist paintings and Leon Bakst's scenery for Diaghilev's ballet. Leontes' palace had very up-to-date art deco architecture, and the pastoral scene took place before a Charles Rennie Mackintosh cottage. The costumes by Albert Rothenstein were based on Giulio Romano—or at least they were claimed to be: Hermione in Figure 5.23 has about as much to do with Giulio Romano as...well, as Paulina's statue. But the claim, the invocation of the magic name, was obviously of the essence. Both art and anachronism were thereby returned to the heart of the play; the *Sunday Times*' reviewer duly reported that "nothing could be more weird, more Shakespeareanly anachronistic than the costumes...—of barbaric hue, of fantastically poetic design, of joy and fastidiousness." The satyr in

Figure 5.23    Albert Rutherston (i.e., Rothenstein),
costume design for Hermione in *The Winter's Tale*,
Savoy Theatre, 1912.

*Figure 5.24* A satyr in *The Winter's Tale*, Savoy Theatre, 1912.

Figure 5.24, however, all too decently outfitted, reveals just how much of a problem Giulio Romano still was in 1912—Diaghilev's audiences got to see a good deal more of Nijinsky's faun. Nevertheless, even for unsympathetic critics the production came as both a revelation and a relief.

More productions would merely reveal more of the same. But suppose we wanted to invent an authentic Giulio Romano sculpture, what would it look like? No doubt something like the exquisite painting of *Ceres* in Plate 16, now in the Louvre, an appropriate model for the nurturing and redemptive mother of a redeemed daughter who models herself on Proserpina—appropriate, but also, in defiance of Shakespeare's text, a maternal image exhibiting no wrinkles, no trace of age or sorrow, sexually suggestive and eternally desirable: it is, after all, by Giulio Romano. The painting is based on an ancient statue of Venus Genitrix, which Giulio owned—the subtext of Giulio's image of

*Figure* 5.25    Giovanni da Udine, Festoon in the Loggia of Psyche, Farnesina Chigi, Rome.

maternal care and grief is the goddess of both lust and love. Would such a statue perhaps also remind us of what always lurks on the margins of Giulio's classicism—in Figure 5.25, for example, at the edge of the legend of Psyche in the Farnesina? Or is this always in the back of Leontes' and Florizel's—and Hermione's and Perdita's and our—minds too?

# Six

## Imagining Shylock

My final example concerns the intersection of history, stage history, and interpretation in the development of a Shakespearean character who has grown, since the eighteenth century, increasingly resonant and disturbing. Shylock is conventionally identified as an outsider in The Merchant of Venice, though generally as a prelude to observing how he also embodies all the essential Venetian qualities. I shall not question what seems to me a critical truism, but I do want to consider what kind of outsider he is, and what it means to be either an insider or an outsider in the world The Merchant of Venice presents. If Venice was an exotic locale to Shakespeare, it is for us a familiar enough place, easily fitting a number of modern models—of early capitalism, of evolving notions of finance, of the beginnings of modern racial stereotyping—as well as some less familiar ones, such as those of the largely fictitious ideal Renaissance republican society, and of English law at a moment of accelerating change in concepts of both equity and citizenship. It is also a truism that the Venice of the Rialto and the dogana is really Shakespeare's London, but here surely the distinctions are more important than the similarities. The Italian setting is everything Elizabethan middle-class mercantile London is not for Shakespeare: a world of romance, glamor, poetry, and danger.

If Shylock is an outsider, what kind of outsider is he? In English and American productions since the late nineteenth century, he has been for the most part a member of a recognizable underclass, often speaking, even in productions with Italian Renaissance settings, with London East End or New York Lower East Side Jewish intonations—that is, not an outsider at all, just the insider we prefer not to know. Before that, from the beginning of the eighteenth century (which is as far back as our records go), he was first, as played by Thomas Dogget, a comic character—this was in George Granville's adaptation, called, significantly, *The Jew of Venice*, the only form in which the play survived the Restoration. As the title attested, the comic villain here was the center of the play. Charles Macklin, starting in the 1740s, and returning, more or less, to Shakespeare's text, was the first performer to conceive Shylock as a tragic figure, in this case a terrifying villain with no redeeming features, eaten up with malice and vindictiveness, a counterpart to Iago, the villain of the other Venetian play. Macklin's "badge of all our tribe" was a red beard, conventional for stage Jews; the "Jewish gaberdine," the rough wool robe that sets him off from the high fashion of his Venetian clients, was a cloak covering unfashionably wide black trousers, and he wore a red skullcap

*Figure 6.1*    Charles Macklin as Shylock, *c.* 1760.

(Figure 6.1). Pope, who saw the performance on its third night, was puzzled by the skullcap and questioned Macklin about it. The actor claimed it as a gesture toward historical accuracy: he explained that he had read that sixteenth-century Venetian Jews did in fact wear red skullcaps, and Pope, suitably impressed, is said to have composed a distich on the subject: "This is the Jew/ That Shakespeare drew." In fact, in various parts of sixteenth-century Italy Jews were required to wear *yellow* hats—Macklin was misinformed on two counts. I shall return to the source of Macklin's information and its implications.

The transformation to the sympathetic Shylock, psychologically human and essentially a martyr to Christian intolerance, was the work of Edmund Kean. Kean's Shylock was far less localized than Macklin's had been, a victim but not recognizably an outsider. It was not until Henry Irving's Shylock at the end of the century, with Ellen Terry as Portia, that the Jew was rationalized geographically, in this case as oriental—though Irving believed Shylock probably came from Frankfurt, he said he had based his interpretation on Jews he had seen in Morocco, "magnificent" Jews.[1] (Figure 6.2). London Jews for once were off the hook: the Jew was at last an authentic outsider. Subsequently, however, he was generally played closer to home, whether as an East End Jew or, starting in the 1930s, an east European refugee, instantly identifiable by his accent, and costumed essentially as a used clothing peddlar—the Jewish gaberdine itself was often distinctly seedy. Shylock the banker, for all his ready money, remained the thoroughly déclassé Jew, the Jew one had necessary dealings with but didn't recognize socially—this throughout two centuries of Rothschilds, Salomons, Montefiores, Warburgs, Sassoons in the London financial world, to say nothing of Rachel, Beerbohm Tree, Pinero, Sarah Bernhardt, Ada Reeve, and Leslie Howard on the London stage. For modern Shylocks, the great watershed production was Jonathan Miller's in 1970, in which Olivier's Shylock was a high Victorian banker—a stroke of genius that made sense out of Portia's question "Which is the merchant here, and which the Jew?" by presenting a Shylock basically indistinguishable from Antonio, a thoroughly British financier, his gaberdine as fine as Antonio's worsted, recognizable as a Jew only when he removed his top hat to reveal his (quite inauthentic and anachronistic) skullcap. Even in this production, even with a thoroughly assimilated, incontestably successful Jewish director, it was necessary to invoke the secret Chasid beneath the English gentleman.

The issue of how to play Shylock is significant because in the history of performance, the Merchant who is the play's titular subject tends to get lost—George Granville's adaptation was in this respect acutely perceptive. The play is, even in the Revels accounts, called *The Jew of Venice*, and though

*Figure 6.2*    Henry Irving as Shylock, 1879.

the most famous actor of the era where our records begin, Betterton (at the age of sixty-six!), played the romantic lead Bassanio, the starring roles—definitively so since Macklin—have always been Shylock and Portia. As for the Merchant, he is not even the second lead; Venice, for the stage, belongs to Shylock, not Antonio. What, then, is an outsider?

Let us return now to Macklin's red skullcap. He almost certainly found it in Coryate. Here is the passage:

> [The Venetian Jews] are distinguished and discerned from the Christians by their habits on their heads; for some of them doe weare hats and those redde, onely those Jewes that are borne in the westerne parts of the world, as in Italy, &c. but the easterne Jewes being otherwise called the Levantine Jewes, which are borne in Hierusalem, Alexandria, Constantinople, &c. weare Turbents upon their heads as the Turkes do.[2]

Note that these are *hats*, not caps. The caps only appear later, when Coryate attends a service at the synagogue and observes that the rabbi is "discerned from the lay people onely by wearing of a redde cap, whereas the others doe weare redde hats."[3] Note too that these Jews are *not* outsiders, they are the Italian Jews; the outsiders, the Levantine Jews, wear turbans.

Shylock is clearly not a rabbi at prayer. Why then did Macklin wear a skullcap, rather than the hat stipulated by his source? Because by the 1740s, the skullcap was a marker of Jews in England. The routine wearing of the skullcap by Jews in fact was an innovation; it dates from the eighteenth century, and was practiced only among orthodox Ashkenazim, Jews from the German tradition. Its point was to devise a dress code specifically differentiating Jews from gentiles, for whom uncovering the head was a sign of respect; it was based on the Christian practice, and designed as a distinguishing alternative. By the mid-eighteenth century it would have been noticeable among Dutch and German Jews trading in London. Macklin's skullcap was in fact not history but sociology, and his performing style too was considered authentically Jewish. According to a report in *The Connoisseur* in 1754,

> he made daily visits to the centre of business, the 'change and the adjacent coffee houses, that by a frequent intercourse and conversation with the "unforeskinned race" he might habituate himself to their air and deportment.[4]

Despite Macklin's claim to Pope, then, his audience recognized him neither as historically correct nor Venetian, but as an authentic contemporary Jew.

Pope's question, then, must have been not about the skullcap but about its color. Why is the skullcap *red*? The decor of Shylock's orthodoxy was thus brought into keeping with his Jewish red hair; but the cap would have had a deeper, if unacknowledged, significance. The production as a whole was costumed in modern dress—Pope might well have wondered why Shylock should have been the only historically correct Venetian—and for Macklin's audience the red skullcap was the badge not of Jews, but of cardinals of the Roman Catholic church. Paradoxical as this juxtaposition sounds, it is probably the only point at which Macklin's conception of the play had a real historical validity, and I shall return to it.

Shylock's Jewishness is insisted on throughout the play; it serves, indeed, as a principle of explanation for his character, and of justification for his treatment at Portia's hands. The play's antisemitism is regularly accounted for by invoking the notorious case of Roderigo Lopez, a physician of Portuguese Jewish descent, who was executed in 1594 on charges of spying and plotting to poison the queen. The relevance of the case to the play was first discussed by Sir Sidney Lee in 1880, and has since appeared almost axiomatic. Since its relevance seems to me, on the contrary, both dubious and farfetched, I shall give, very briefly, an account of this complex and confusing affair. Lopez was a respected and successful doctor. He may have been born in England—there were physicians named Lopez in England from the time of Henry VIII—but in any case, he was there by 1559, and by 1569 was a member of the College of Physicians. In the 1570s he was attending first Walsingham, the head of the Elizabethan secret service, and then the Earl of Leicester, Elizabeth's chief minister. In 1586 he became the queen's chief physician. He was not a Jew, except in the sense defined by the Nuremberg laws; he was either descended from converts or a convert himself, and was a regular communicant in the Anglican church. (Gabriel Harvey, who disliked him, described him as "descended of Jewes: but himself A Christian.")[5] Before his trial he was occasionally referred to as a Jew, but this may well have been considered an asset, establishing his expertise in one of the few professions open to Jews and in which they were acknowledged to excel. Even when the charge is hostile, it is also admiring, as in a passage in the scurrilous pamphlet *Leicester's Commonwealth*, published in 1584, which lists Leicester's agents "for divers affairs": "two Galenists for agents in the university: Dee and Allen (two atheists) for figuring and conjuring: Julio the Italian & Lopez the Jew, for poisoning, and for the art of destroying children in women's bellies...."[6] Jews are among the experts.

As a Portuguese speaker with connections in high places, however, his usefulness was not limited to his medical skills. He was a logical person to install as adviser and interpreter to Don Antonio, the chief claimant to the Portuguese crown, who was for a few years a key figure in Walsingham's and Essex's anti-Spanish machinations. Portugal had been annexed by Philip II of Spain in 1581, on the death of the Portuguese king, and Don Antonio spent a fruitless decade in Paris and London seeking support for his claim. Essex talked of leading a Spanish invasion to place Antonio on the Portuguese throne, but it eventually became clear that the project had less to do with Portugal than with Essex's plans for his own advancement, and Antonio, blaming Lopez for misleading him, dismissed his adviser. Essex had also employed Lopez to deal with Spanish agents, hoping thereby to lure the Spanish king into some action that would justify open warfare against Spain, with himself as the heroic general. The Spanish duly proposed a payment to Lopez of 50,000 ducats— £18,000, a gigantic sum in the period—if he would poison the queen. Lopez agreed, but demanded payment in advance; the matter went no further. In all this, of course, Lopez was acting on Essex's orders.

The whole scheme fell apart when Lopez revealed some part of it to the queen, who had no interest in a war with Spain, and had a showdown with Essex over the business. Essex was understandably furious, and in any case had no further use for Lopez. Two underlings were got to confess that Lopez had discussed the poisoning plot with them, and had had more correspondence with Spain than he had revealed to his employers; and though a search of Lopez's house produced nothing incriminating, he was threatened with torture and confessed to plotting against the queen's life. Tried for high treason by a court headed by Essex, he was found guilty, and sentenced to death. The queen for many months refused to sign the death warrant, and after the execution was finally carried out returned his fortune to his widow. Camden, who was not an eyewitness, later claimed that Lopez had cried from the scaffold that he loved the queen more than he loved Jesus Christ, to which the crowd replied "He is a Jew, he is a Jew." This is exceedingly improbable, and Camden is the only source for the story, but even as it stands there is nothing disingenuous about such an assertion from Lopez: he was in fact a practicing Anglican. It is more likely, however, that he was subsequently declared a Jew as a further justification for his execution.

To represent him as a Jew, in fact, was not a significant part of the prosecutorial rhetoric, if indeed it was present at all. Robert Cecil reported that at his trial Lopez was condemned as a "murdering traitor and Jewish doctor...worse than Judas himself," and that the judge referred to him as "that vile Jew."[7] But this too seems to be a later addition to the story, recorded in none of the records of the trial; and in the longest and most widely circulated account of the affair, a pamphlet called *A True Report of Sundry Horrible Conspiracies* published in November 1594, which gives a very detailed if confused narrative of the case, the fact that he is a Jew is nowhere mentioned. The tract is all about Lopez's dealings with Spanish agents, and his part in the international Jesuit conspiracy. The case is most interesting in its ambivalences: Lopez is of course assumed to be machiavellian and untrustworthy; but he is being used by the English throughout. And though Essex was surely justified in feeling that Lopez had betrayed his confidence, it was to the queen that Lopez had betrayed it, and he did so because his loyalty to the queen was greater than his loyalty to Essex—the queen herself perceived this, and protected Lopez until the weight of judicial pressure and public opinion made it impossible to do so any longer. The charge of villainy and betrayal obviously contains a lot of psychological projection in it: the machiavel here really is Essex, and the unforgivable crime is that he has been exposed.

What has all this to do with Shylock? Not much—readers of *Sundry Horrible Conspiracies* would not even have been aware that Lopez was a Jew. Being a Jew here is tantamount to being an agent of the papacy and a tool of the Jesuits—this is the sense in which Macklin's red skullcap has a real historical validity. The case does, however, seem to have a tangential relevance to Marlowe's Jew, who claims to go around poisoning people. *The Jew of Malta* was probably written in 1589 or 1590, and the first recorded performance was in 1592, long before Lopez was an available model; but the play was performed twice within ten days of the execution, in June 1594, and this is unlikely to have been coincidental. That *The Merchant of Venice*, written in 1596 or 1597, has something to do with Marlowe's play is not a matter for dispute. Jay Halio points out that *The Jew of Malta* was performed by the Lord Admiral's Men, the rivals of Shakespeare's company, eight times in 1596, and *The Merchant* was doubtless designed to capitalize on its continuing popularity.[8] In short, Shylock is a Jew not because Lopez was, but because Barabas was.

But what kind of Jew is Shylock? Barabas is identifiable as a reprehensible Jew simply from his name, that of the biblical thief released instead of Jesus. Shakespeare's other Jews, too, have immediately recognizable biblical names: Leah, Tubal, Chus (or Cush in the Authorized Version); but Shylock and Jessica come from another onomastic world entirely. Commentators since the eighteenth century have been baffled by Shylock's name, and have attempted to rationalize it by deriving it from Shiloh, a word for the Messiah, or from a genealogy in Genesis where the name Shelah is found, or from a pamphlet entitled *Caleb Shillocke his prophecy, or the Jew's Prediction* which, since it was published in 1607, is more likely to derive from Shakespeare's Shylock than Shylock from it. The point of all this critical energy is to avoid the awkward fact that Shylock is, quite simply, an English name—this was first pointed out in 1849 by M. A. Lower, who found a power of attorney granted to a Sir Richard Shylok of Hoo, Sussex, in 1435. Subsequent commentators looking for keys to Shakespeare dismissed Sir Richard Shylok because he had no evident connection with either Shakespeare or usury, as if he were the only person in England who ever bore that surname. But Sir Richard Shylok had ancestors, and siblings, and relatives, and descendants; and over several hundred years there were other Shylock families who were not related to him. The surname Shylock appears in the hundreds rolls, and the name had been, since Saxon times, a native one. It means white haired, and is the same name as its more common English equivalents Whitlock and Whitehead. The original name is still in use: there is a Christopher Shylock currently living in London, and the Shylock Beauty Salon may be found in Sydney. Shylock is not some form of a biblical name; in Shakespeare's time it was clearly and unambiguously English.

As for Jessica, it too is not a biblical name, though unlike Shylock, it is also not English. It might be like Sidney's Pamela, an invented name that has passed into the culture. Pamela, however, reveals its sources easily: all honey, or sweetness, or melody. Jessica is less easy to locate. It might conceivably be intended as a female diminutive of the name of David's father Jesse, which would be appropriate because Jesse means "wealth"; but there is no reason whatever to believe that Shakespeare knew any Hebrew or was being advised by someone who did. Attempts to extract Jessica more directly from the Old Testament are even more farfetched. They depend on a brief genealogy of Abraham's family in Genesis 11.29, in which a daughter is mentioned whose name is given in the Geneva Bible as Iscah and in the Bishops' Bible as Jisca, and who is never referred to again. But surely in the world of Leah, Tubal and Cush, this is clutching at straws: Jessica is in fact a common enough name in Scotland, a diminutive of the woman's name Jessie. If Shakespeare knew any Jessicas they were Scottish.

What does this mean? To begin with, it may reveal more about us than about Shakespeare. There are many parallels. The Navarre of *Love's Labour's Lost* includes Nathaniel and Costard (the most English of apples); all the Athenian workmen in *A Midsummer Night's Dream* have English names—Snout, Bottom, Snug, Quince, Flute, Starveling; the Mediterranean duchy of Illyria is home to the relentlessly English Sir Toby Belch and Sir Andrew Aguecheek; the servants in the Verona of *Romeo and Juliet* are Sampson, Gregory, Peter and Abraham (and no critic to my knowledge has ever claimed that Sampson and Abraham were Jews); the villain in *Much Ado About Nothing*, a world of Pedros, Leonatos, Claudios, Borachios, is Don John. Shakespeare often wanted his clowns and grotesques to be recognizably English—why is only Shylock's name a problem?

Where do we go from there? If I were hunting for the real Shylock of Shakespeare's imagination, I would look not in Old Testament genealogies but in the continuing Elizabethan debates on banking and interest—for example, in Thomas Wilson's *Discourse Upon Usury* (1572), and more particularly in R. H. Tawney's masterful long introduction to the 1925 edition. The Shylocks of Shakespeare's world were absolutely ubiquitous; but by the end of the sixteenth century they began to be localized in a few groups: goldsmiths, mercers, and most visibly of all, scriveners, who combined the functions of accountant and legal adviser. None of these had anything to do with Jews—the association of Jews with usury in England was entirely conventional. Wilson, on the contrary, is convinced that the rise of usury was precisely a function of Protestantism, of Reformation morality and the abandonment of canon law. As Tawney says, "Calvin approached [economic life] as a man of affairs, who assumed, as the starting point of his social theory, capital, credit, large-scale enterprise,"[9] and therefore sanctioned the taking of interest on loans.

So one way to play Shylock "authentically" would be as one of the Puritan moneylenders of Shakespeare's London, for whom the Old Testament rhetoric would be entirely in character, and the Jewishness a moral comment on the profession. I am not, however, looking for a "real" Shylock, I am simply following out the implications of his English name. What about the fact that he is a Jew: what would an authentic Jew be like for Shakespeare's stage? To begin with, not a lower-class Londoner or an east European refugee with a yarmulke, but Spanish or Portuguese: such figures carried with them, as in the Lopez case, the villainous subtext of Jesuit subversion. James Shapiro cites a wonderfully paranoid passage from William Prynne that makes the point: "If extraordinary care be not taken...under pretext of Jews, we shall have many hundreds of Jesuits, Popish priests, and friars come over freely into England from Portugal, Spain, Rome, Italy, and other places, under the title, habit, and disguise of Jews."[10] The Jew is the mask of the papist—we return to Macklin's red skullcap.

To play Shylock as a Renaissance Spaniard would not, of course, have much resonance for a modern audience. To play him as a modern Latino, however, would make a striking kind of sense for American audiences: Shylock, after all, is not an outsider, any more than Latinos are in American society. He is as Venetian as the Christians are, but he is part of an underclass, marginalized within the society. Latinos are not associated with money in our culture, but a production might make real capital out of that. After all, if, as Antonio says, there are Christian moneylenders who charge no interest, then why are Bassanio and Antonio involved with Shylock at all? But the point is surely that Bassanio has already gone to all the classy mainline banks, and none of them will give him the time of day—Antonio is obviously a bad risk, and his emissary is an even worse one. So he ends up with Shylock—that means, let's say, in our American production, that he ends up at a barrio bank. The Latino banker also sees perfectly well that Antonio and Bassanio are a bad investment, but he never gets any business from the Anglo community, and he thinks that if he does a favor for Antonio perhaps that will get him some clout in the mainstream financial world—at least Antonio will be in his debt, owe him some favors. So he makes the loan, with a jokey stipulation substituting a body part for his usual interest—a joke, that is, that precludes his charging interest. And then he gets completely screwed by the Anglo world he is trying to become a part of, losing not just his money but his daughter to the Anglos, and he goes crazy and gets very vindictive. That would be, for us, a quite comprehensible psychological scenario.

But as I have already suggested, there is another side to Shylock, and to the Jew figure, for the Elizabethans, and that is his Old Testament component. Jews have a special status theologically: they are neither heathens nor heretics, categorically different from pagans and Moslems because they were God's chosen people, and in them Renaissance Christianity saw its own past. The conversion of the Jews was a holy mission, because it would mark the historical completion of Christ's work—the Turks were to be destroyed, but the Jews had to be converted. Coryate expresses the cultural ambivalence very clearly, observing from his Venetian experience that "our English proverbe: To looke like a Jewe (whereby is meant sometimes a weather beaten warp-faced fellow, sometimes a phreneticke and lunaticke person, sometimes one discontented) is not true. For indeed I noted some of them to be most elegant and sweet featured persons, which gave me occasion the more to lament their religion."[11] And for Christians who saw the church as corrupt, or as having fallen away from its proper function and its original purity, the Jews represented a tradition to be embraced and returned to, a way of starting afresh. Various radical Protestant sects used the Jews as a model, both for the ordering of society and for their rhetoric; and there is a lot in Shylock's language that recalls Puritan ways of speaking and arguing. Such sects quite explicitly emulated Judaism, calling their priests rabbis and using Hebrew— Jonson satirizes the practice with Rabbi Zeal-of-the-Land Busy in *Bartholomew Fair*. In 1655 Cromwell convened the Whitehall Conference to discuss formally readmitting the Jews to England—they had been formally expelled in 1290. There were even negotiations to sell the decaying St Paul's Cathedral to the Jewish community as a great central synagogue, and while the Whitehall Conference ended inconclusively, the government granted various privileges to resident Jews, though it stopped short of allowing them to be naturalized. They were technically "denizens," legally resident in the society but not finally integrated into it.

Shylock can be seen as a kind of Puritan. Shakespeare is not at all sympathetic to the Puritan cause, but his distaste for it is not a distaste for foreigners. Shylock is very deeply part of Venetian society; he expresses a good deal of its deepest nature. The success of both Antonio's love for Bassanio and Bassanio's love for Portia depends not only on Shylock's capital, but on his willingness to see it used merely to enable a Venetian romance. This helps to explain the strange ambivalence Shakespeare exhibits about this villain; and it also helps to explain why he is unwilling to destroy or expel him after the trial scene, but wants to incorporate him into the Christian world, to force him to convert. He is an essential part of Venice, which is to say, of England. Hence the most striking point about him, his English name: there is Shakespeare's ambivalence epitomised. Just what kind of subversion does this figure represent? All those pleasure-loving types in the play are Italians, but for an Elizabethan audience, Shylock is one of us.

The other side of this, of course, is the continuing, corrosive, paranoid antisemitism so thoroughly chronicled and analyzed by James Shapiro. The most dangerous aspect of Jews was precisely how much like "us" they were, the fear that they were in fact indistinguishable, that anyone might be a secret Jew. The telltale sign of circumcision was, after all, to any but the most intimate of observers, invisible, and for women there was no sign whatever. Shapiro cites a fascinating fantasy of a minister named Josselin in Essex in 1655, who had dreamt that "one came to me and told me that Thurloe [Oliver Cromwell's Secretary of State] was turned Jew; I answered perhaps it was a mistake, he might declare he was a Jew born, the Jews having lived here, and he pretend by old writings his pedigree from them, to ingratiate with the Jews, or some compliance with them." Shapiro asks,

> What are we to make of Josselin's response in his dream that news of John Thurloe's conversion was "a mistake"? Not that this report was false, but that Thurloe was not really "turned Jew"; rather, he was simply pretending to be "a Jew born" for politic reasons. It is not entirely clear what it means here to "turn" Jew. Is this something one chooses to do, or is it somehow beyond one's control? Have religious or national identity become so unstable as to be vulnerable to such an unlikely transformation? Perhaps the most interesting feature of the dream is Josselin's notion that Thurloe would defend this claim by reinventing his "pedigree" through antiquarian records, "old writings" connecting his lineage back to the Jews who, centuries earlier, had lived in England. Here was the repressed returning with a vengeance.[12]

The baffling question here of why one would choose to be a Jew, or to represent oneself as one, however, conceals a deeper and more disturbing question: how can one ever know who is a Jew and who is not? Indeed, if one traced one's own impeccably British ancestors far enough back, one might find Jews among them, "the Jews having lived here," as Josselin says. In this fantasy, the very wellspring of British history is contaminated with the alien presence. One might, then, "really" be a Jew oneself and not know it: the question of what it means "really" to be a Jew remained unanswerable. Is it a matter of lineage, of belief, of practice? Is someone who does not perform Jewish rituals, pray as a Jew, profess the faith—someone like Dr Lopez, for example—"really" a Jew? Is an uncircumcised Jew (like Daniel Deronda) "really" a Jew? In Jewish law, Jewish identity passes through the mother; the child of a Jewish father and a gentile mother is not a Jew. This of course makes the racial identification even more problematic, since the woman bears no sign of her religion—Jessica says her husband has made her a Christian, but is this the case? Can a Jewish woman become Christian?

What will be the status of her children then—are they Jewish or gentile? If "Jewish blood" is involved, does a change in belief affect the blood line? In fact, a child may be either Jewish or gentile depending on whether one applies the Mosaic or the patriarchal law. Those who are Jews to the English may not be Jews to the Jews.

For Shakespeare's England, the fantasy of secret contamination is not at all limited to the Jews; but the Jews provide an essential model. In *Titus Andronicus*, when Tamora gives birth to Aaron's black child, the villainous Moor, never at a loss for a stratagem, determines to substitute another:

> Not far, one Muliteus, my countryman,
> His wife but yesternight was brought to bed.
> His child is like to her, fair as you are. (4.2.153–5)

This is the same fantasy even more racially charged, a testimony to the impossibility of determining not only whether one's child is one's own, but even whether it is "really" white or black: blackness in this case is not at all a function of skin color. It is surely not coincidental that Aaron is the name of the brother of Moses.

How does all the ambivalence about Shylock, the tragic energy, the dangerous and subversive potential, get accommodated to comedy—why is it an element in comedy at all? The idea that comedy and tragedy are not opposites but complements is not a new one—at the end of the *Symposium* Socrates tells Agathon and Aristophanes, tragic and comic playwrights, that their crafts are the same, and every Shakespeare comedy, from *The Comedy of Errors* to *The Tempest*, has its tragic elements. What distinguishes comedy from tragedy is not the problems they act out, but what they accept as solutions. Many commentators have remarked the similarities between Shylock and that stock figure of the Italian comedy the pantaloon. Pantalone is the heavy father, morbidly protective of his daughter Columbine. Sixteenth- and seventeenth-century depictions of him might be depictions of the original Shylock: he is elderly, has a hooked nose, and carries a large knife in his belt (See Figure 6.3.) Irascible and vindictive, he is driven wild by Columbine's flirtations with Harlequin and other young men. Making off with his daughter and his ducats is no more than a condign punishment, an entirely predictable comic conclusion. What is missing from this as a model for Shylock is, obviously, a complex psychology, an explanatory history, a credible motivation—in short, Shakespeare—but it is difficult to imagine Shylock without Pantalone somewhere in the background.

But comic or tragic, does Shylock in fact sum up the play's threatening potential? After the trial scene, after the tragic plot has been resolved, the play nevertheless still includes an insistent sense of danger, ominous overtones

*Figure 6.3*    Pantalone, from *Compositions de Rhetorique de M. Don Arlequin* (Lyons, 1601), a parodic rhetoric.

that derive not from Shylock but precisely from the conventions of comedy itself, the complexities of courtship and the promise—and, in Shakespeare, the very ominous implications—of marriage. Shylock both is and is not part of that structure, and banishing him or converting him does not remove him. In one way, as I have said, he is essential to it: his money is required for the success of Bassanio's love for Portia and of Antonio's love for Bassanio, because that is an essential relationship in the play too. But what is essential, it turns out, is also subversive: the translation of love into money, money into love, is not a simple matter. It remains benign only so long as money can be thought of merely as *riches*—as in the case of Portia, the lady richly left: she *has* her money, she doesn't *make* it. As soon as money is conceived to be finance, however, the essence of commerce, venture capital, capital in the Marxist sense, it becomes threatening both to love and to that sense of self that love depends on—it controls us, instead of our controlling it. Hence the dangers of choosing the gold or silver caskets. What Venice requires also undermines it.

Most critical treatments of the play until very recently have said that it ends with heavenly harmony, and the happy marriages of Portia and Bassanio, Nerissa and Gratiano, Lorenzo and Jessica. But in fact, most of the fifth act is taken up with the consequences of Portia's ring trick. This is commonly either dismissed as a joke, if a rather malicious one, or defended as a way of insisting on the primacy of marriage over all other relationships. But it has implications that have little to do with harmony, least of all the harmony of marriage. To begin with, the women have made their husbands' love equivalent to the rings they have given them. This is the same translation Othello does with Desdemona's handkerchief and Posthumus does with Imogen's bracelet, and if Othello and Posthumus are at fault so are Portia and Nerissa: the material basis of love is as powerful at the play's conclusion as at its beginning, and as powerful in this comedy as it is in Shakespearean tragedy. The model of marriage here, moreover, is that of Shylock: he had a ring from Leah when he was a bachelor; he would not have given it up for a wilderness of monkeys.

The test of the men's faith is both a trap and exceedingly revealing about the nature of marriage in the play. Portia and Nerissa know perfectly well that Bassanio and Gratiano have not given the rings as love tokens to other women, but as a compelled recompense for an overwhelming debt of gratitude to two young men. The whole reason the women disguise themselves as men, rather than coming to the court in their own persons or disguised as other women, is precisely that this is the only way to get the rings away from their husbands. Other women have nothing to do with the matter, and they know it. Nor are they even really concerned about other women: the principal point of the charade, though this is unacknowledged, is to separate Bassanio from Antonio. What the ruse does beyond this, and what it is specifically designed to do, is give the wives a grudge to hold over their husbands for ever—this is what the primacy of marriage depends on, this is the reason that husbands should be faithful. Of course, if their husbands' interest in either young men or older admirers is really a significant menace, if this is really the danger the grudge is a prophylactic against, then keeping any number of rings safe will hardly ensure the sanctity of the marriage vow.

The blatant materialism of the play's conclusion is surely part of its point: Portia's money has rescued Bassanio, just as Shylock's has done, and however clever, charming or beautiful Portia is, both Bassanio and the play itself make it quite clear from the outset that she is nothing to him without money— "In Belmont is a lady richly left.../ And many Jasons come in quest of her" (1.1.161–72). This Jason does indeed obtain the golden fleece: but does he also marry Medea? The insistent sense of threat and danger no doubt accounts for the fact that, for all its high romance, the play has been, as far back as our records take us, a play about Shylock; many productions, over the years, have simply ended the play with the trial scene. Ask people who the merchant of Venice is, and nine out of ten will reply that it is Shylock. But the play, nominally at least, is about Antonio, and the threat posed by Shylock to his lavish altruism, which is the path to love. As a summary of the play, however, this does not quite do it; because if Antonio is necessary to the successful outcome of love in the play, so is Shylock—Antonio's money is Shylock's money; there is no Antonio without Shylock. Credit, bonds, trust, above all cash, are central to the worlds of both Venice and Belmont—the loan is not incidental, and you cannot have love without money.

Venice, then, contains its own dangers: it is not only Shylock who presents us with tragic possibilities; those tragic implications exist even without Shylock. If we look at the play symbolically, we might say that Shylock sums up the destructive tendencies of both Venice and Belmont—the overwhelming concern with money, the literalizing of bonds, whether Shylock's bond or Portia's ring, the emphasis on the flesh, not on the spirit. Why does Shylock ask for a pound of flesh nearest the heart? Obviously not for any reason having to do with character, but precisely because the flesh is what is closest to the heart.

Even in overcoming its dangers and signaling its romantic triumphs, the play has a kind of overkill. In the love scene between Lorenzo and Jessica at the opening of Act 5, the lovers are finally free, and together, and rich; and they have the support of the most powerful people in their world. How do they celebrate their victory? They entertain each other with mythological stories of tragic love affairs: the faithless Cressida, suicidal Thisbe, betrayed Dido, murderous Medea—and then themselves: the extravagant, untrustworthy Lorenzo; the rash and slanderous Jessica. The disasters of passion, the dangers of the flesh, are the substance of poetry and the resolution of comedy—there is no comedy without tragedy.

Let us turn finally to the triumph over Shylock, the trial scene, with its eulogy on unconstrained mercy. Portia's—or Shakespeare's—behavior toward Antonio is in fact as cruel as anything Shylock does. The scene is drawn out excruciatingly, and its theatrical power has much less to do with the quality of mercy than with the pleasures of sadism on the one hand and revenge on the other. Gratiano, who simply wants to see Shylock drawn and quartered, obviously expresses a good deal of what Shakespeare's audience would have felt—this is a particularly clear case where Shylock and the Venetians are mirror images of each other. Gratiano doesn't get his way, but he gets more of his way than Portia's speech about mercy would lead us to expect. In particular, he gets the deep satisfaction of Portia's invocation of the forgotten law about plots against the lives of Venetian citizens. Shylock has already lost his case on technical grounds: why bring another case against him?

Consider the trial as a whole, and particularly where we stand during it. Suppose Portia had stopped the proceedings at the point where Shylock has lost his case on technicalities: how would the play be changed if, after her close reading of the bond, Shylock were sent home unsatisfied, with Antonio's life intact, and only the return of his principle, or not even that, for comfort? But no, we'd say, that wouldn't do it. He has been too much of a threat; not only the action of the play but his own vindictiveness demand more retribution than that. Gratiano no doubt overstates the case when he is outraged that any mercy at all is being shown to the Jew, but he expresses something that we do feel—that Shylock has to be exorcised, requires a degree of retribution that is not provided for in the mere forfeiture of the pound of flesh. The old law that Portia suddenly invokes allows for this—allows, that is, for us to have our revenge. It also allows for a degree of mercy to be shown to Shylock far greater than any he was willing to extend to Antonio. The law calls for the forfeiture of all his goods and his life; in fact, he keeps half his goods and his life.

But does this really satisfy us, even as Renaissance Christians? There is something deeply problematic about the old law: it is trumped up. No one has ever heard of it before; only Portia knows about it, and she springs it on Shylock, and on all of us, at the last possible moment. After Shylock has lost his case, she reveals that he never had a case at all. The threat against Antonio was never anything but a threat against himself, potential suicide. Anybody can see what the problem with the bond will be; but the old law is a secret, in effect an ex post facto law, which applies only to Shylock, and has been invoked—indeed invented—solely to put him at the mercy of the court. This is a striking example of the play's tendency toward overkill, because the forgotten law is Shakespeare's invention, appearing in none of the sources, and quite unnecessary to the plot.

Viewed in this way, the court's mercy looks rather different. In a scene in which Antonio is allowed nearly to die of fright, Shylock is deprived of half his property and forced to abandon his faith. Does this really constitute mercy? The answer is, it does and it doesn't; it is an utterly ambiguous resolution that satisfies our sadism, our charity and our vindictiveness in the same dramatic moment. It also contributes significantly to the oddly schizoid response that Shylock, in the trial scene in particular, seems to demand of us. Shylock is, unquestionably, the villain of the play; but there is something in the character that we are asked to sympathize with and are unwilling to reject.

In one sense he is antithetical to the altruism of Venice and the generosity of Christianity, but in another he confronts the Venetians with the truth about themselves: that they are versions of him, not only in their essential humanity—"hath not a Jew eyes…"—but in their inhumanity as well:

# The moſt excellent
## Hiſtorie of the *Merchant*
## *of Venice*.

VVith the extreame crueltie of *Shylocke* the Iewe
towards the ſayd Merchant, in cutting a iuſt pound
of his fleſh : and the obtayning of *Portia*
by the choyſe of three
cheſts.

*As it hath beene diuers times acted by the Lord*
*Chamberlaine his Seruants.*

Written by William Shakeſpeare.

AT LONDON,
Printed by *I. R.* for Thomas Heyes,
and are to be ſold in Paules Church-yard, at the
ſigne of the Greene Dragon.
1 6 0 0.

Figure 6.4   Title page, *The Merchant of Venice*, 1600.

> You have among you many a purchased slave
> Which, like your asses and your dogs and mules,
> You use in abject and in slavish parts,
> Because you bought them. Shall I say to you,
> "Let them be free, marry them to your heirs."
> ...You will answer
> "The slaves are ours." So do I answer you.    (4.1.90–8)

This might in fact have touched some nerves—England was heavily involved in the slave trade by the 1590s (Venice was not), and it is not at all clear where an Elizabethan audience's sympathies would have been at this point. Shylock also confronts his audience with their hatred; for Antonio has set the terms of the bond as much as Shylock. Shylock is presented as the heavy, the disapproving father, interfering with our fun, and against whom we naturally rebel. But surely we also feel that he just might be right—and Shakespeare's moralizing culture would have felt it far more strongly. Is Bassanio's extravagance a virtue? Isn't it true that Lorenzo and Jessica are spendthrifts—do we want to see our children (to say nothing of our elders: Antonio is not a child) act that way? After all the parties, won't there be a day of reckoning? When we start thinking in this way, the whole moral structure of the play starts to look different. "Antonio is a good man...": Is Antonio a good man—good in either sense? Would we lend him money? In fact, Shylock agrees to the loan knowing that Antonio is a bad risk: he says he's trying to be friendly. Is Antonio trying to be friendly—is he even willing to try? To which one of the two is it a cold business arrangement? And however romantic we find the fine careless rapture with which Antonio and Bassanio treat their money, do we really believe, in our own lives, that extravagance is a virtue and thrift isn't? And so forth: Shylock touches on profoundly ambivalent attitudes in all of us, and this effect would have been far more powerful to Elizabethan audiences, many of whom were strongly sympathetic to Puritan attitudes.

I conclude my history of Shylock as an inescapable presence both for the play and for England with a bit of originary bibliography. The title page of the first quarto reads, "The Excellent History of *The Merchant of Venice*. With the extreme cruelty of Shylock the Jew towards the said Merchant, in cutting a just pound of his flesh, And the obtaining of Portia by the choice of three caskets. 1600" (see Figure 6.4). This seems to promise a quite different trial scene, in which Shylock is awarded his just pound of flesh, and takes it. The final clause implies that he obtains Portia too. By 1600, the play had already become Shylock's.

# Epilogue

As a summary of the action of *The Merchant of Venice*, the reading proposed by the original title page is doubtless perverse, but it may serve as an appropriately emblematic conclusion to this investigation, in that it so neatly exemplifies the utter dependency of text on interpretation, and accurately foretells the complex and divided history of performance. Increasingly strenuous attempts by playwrights to control the interpretation of their plays, from Jonson's interventionist commentators and printed critical prefaces, to Shaw's novelistic stage directions and disquisitions on what the characters feel, to Genet's, Beckett's, and Arthur Miller's refusal, at times litigious, to allow productions of their plays they deemed unorthodox, only confirm the stubborn independence of the script. By the end of the seventeenth century and until late in the nineteenth, the author was often incorporated into the performing tradition by being made responsible for rehearsals, in effect becoming the director; but even so, it was a rare play that emerged in performance as it had been delivered from the author's pen or appeared in print, and it was a much rarer revival of a play remaining in the repertory that truly replicated the original. The imitation of life is as changeable as life itself.

It is also as transitory. One of the greatest problems of theater history is to see with the eyes of the past. The problem is not only in changing notions of representation—Garrick's pneumatic wig in *Hamlet* derives not from any observation of human behavior, but from a psychology still firmly rooted in mechanistic physiology—but even more in the tendency of history itself to seek explanations in the general rather than the particular, to distrust the individual and exceptional. What audiences want is never a constant, and is determinable by actors, directors and producers, moreover, only through trial and error, and largely in hindsight; and this is true in great measure because the very notion of the audience as a unit with definable tastes and responses is suspect. People have always gone to the theater for the widest variety of reasons, many of which have nothing to do with whatever play happens to be on the stage. Plato decried the immorality of actors and the dishonesty and irrationality of fictions, but for moralists, these have always paled into insignificance beside the infinite and uncontrollable desires of spectators. Having begun with scripts and performers, here is where we must conclude: the essence of drama, the theater's life and soul, is finally the audience.

# Notes

## Chapter One: Imagining Shakespeare

1. G. Blakemore Evans, ed., *Shakespearean Prompt-Books of the Seventeenth Century*, vol. I, the Padua *Macbeth* (Charlottesville: Bibliographical Society of Virginia, 1960); vol. II, the Padua *Measure for Measure* (1963); *The History of King Henry the Fourth as Revised by Sir Edward Dering, Bart.*, eds. George Walton Williams and G. Blakemore Evans (Charlottesville: University Press of Virginia, 1974).
2. Padua *Macbeth*, General Introduction, p. 10.
3. "Rereading the Peacham Drawing," *Shakespeare Quarterly* 50:2 (Summer 1999), pp. 171–84. Schleuter is cautious about identifying the German play, *Eine sehr klägliche Tragœdia von Tito Andronico und der hoffertigen Käserin*, published in a collection of English plays in translation in Leipzig in 1620, with *Titus and Vespasian*, but there is no other *Titus* play known—though *Titus and Vespasian* is admittedly known only by its title.
4. See Paul Sawyer, "Processions and Coronations on the London Stage, 1727–61," *Theatre Notebook* 14:1 (Autumn 1959), pp. 7–12.
5. George C. D. Odell, *Shakespeare from Betterton to Irving* (New York: Charles Scribner's Sons, 1920), vol. 2, p. 169.
6. *The Defence of Poesie* (London, 1595), sig. I1r-v.

## Chapter Two: Staging Clio

1. I am indebted to Richard Schoch for calling this example to my attention.
2. "The Horrors of *King Lear*," *The Kenyon Review* 11:2 (spring, 1949), pp. 348–50.
3. Princeton University Press, 1983, and Cambridge University Press, 1998.
4. George C. D. Odell, *Shakespeare from Betterton to Irving*. (New York: Charles Scribner's Sons 1920), vol. 1, p. 340. Odell greatly understates the extent of Garrick's revisions.
5. At 5.3.131 Coriolanus reveals that he has been seated by rising with the words "I have sat too long"; at 5.4.21–2 he is compared to a statue of Alexander on his throne.
6. Moelwyn Merchant, *Shakespeare and the Artist* (London: Oxford University Press, 1959), p. 140.
7. W. Graham Robertson, *Time Was* (London: H. Hamilton, 1931), p. 151.

## Chapter Three: History and Biography

1. There is a large body of literature on this subject, and it will be evident that I disagree with much of it. The work of David Piper is essential, despite the fact that he believes in the Chandos portrait: see especially *The Image of the Poet* (Oxford: Clarendon Press, 1982), and the pamphlet *O Sweet Mr. Shakespeare I'll Have His Picture* (London: National Portrait Gallery, 1964). The question of portraiture is peripheral to Margreta de Grazia's concerns in *Shakespeare Verbatim* (Oxford:

Clarendon Press, 1991), but her chapter on portraiture is superb. And all of Michael Dobson's *The Making of the National Poet* (Oxford: Clarendon Press, 1992) is relevant.

2. Indeed, so problematic has the portrait seemed that it has been doubted that Droeshout the Younger can have been responsible for it, or that he even was an engraver. Mary Edmond, "It was for gentle Shakespeare cut," *Shakespeare Quarterly* 42, no. 3 (1991), pp. 339–44, argues energetically that the folio engraver was in fact Droeshout's uncle, Martin Droeshout the elder; but since there is no surviving work by this artist with which to compare the Shakespeare portrait, the claim is speculative at best. Edmond also claims that there is no documentary evidence for the younger Droeshout as an engraver, or indeed, at all after his birth record in 1601. Christian Schuckman, however, in "The engraver of the first folio portrait of William Shakespeare," *Print Quarterly* 8, no. 1 (1991), pp. 40–43—obviously published too late for Edmond to take it into account—shows that the younger Droeshout emigrated to Spain in the late 1620s, and reproduces a number of engravings done by him there. One of these bears a striking similarity to the Shakespeare portrait, and leaves little doubt that Martin the younger is the folio's Droeshout. The explanation for his elusiveness is apparently simply that he was Catholic, and found more patrons in Catholic Spain.

3. New York, Viking Press, p. 310.

4. 3.1; cited in *Shakespeare Allusion Book*, ed. John Munro (London: Oxford University Press, 1932), vol. 1, p. 68.

5. *Aubrey's Brief Lives*, ed. O. L. Dick (Ann Arbor: University of Michigan Press, 1957), p. 85.

6. See S. Schoenbaum, *William Shakespeare: Records and Images* (London and New York: Oxford University Press, 1981), pp. 160–61.

## Chapter Four: Magic and History

1. "Shaping Fantasies," *Representations* 2 (1983), pp. 61–94.

2. I quote from Sir Thomas North's Elizabethan translation, which Shakespeare used. Cited in Harold F. Brooks' Arden *A Midsummer Night's Dream* (London: Methuen, 1979), p. 136.

3. Introduction, p. 73.

4. London, 1587, fols. 3v–4r.

5. Philip Stubbes, *Anatomy of Abuses*, 1585, fol. L8v.

6. E.g., Stephen Gossen, *The Schoole of Abuse* (1579), p. 10.

7. E. K. Chambers, *William Shakespeare* (Oxford: Clarendon Press, 1930), 1:362.

8. *Newes from Scotland*, in G. B. Harrison, ed., James I, *Daemonologie and Newes From Scotland* (Bodley Head Quartos, 1924), p. 14. Quotations from this text are modernized.

9. Ibid., pp. 21–23.

10. She is confused at one point with another witch named Agnis Sampson, apparently a misprint, though the association of witchcraft with the hero whose downfall came from his attraction to heathen and emasculating women is worth remarking.

11. Ibid., p. 15.

12. For a discussion of James's attacks on women as an index both to his relations with his mother and his sense of himself, see Jonathan Goldberg, *James I and the Politics of Literature* (Baltimore: Johns Hopkins University Press, 1983), pp. 24–25. The most detailed consideration of James's homoerotic liaisons is David M. Bergeron's *King James and Letters of Homoerotic Desire* (Iowa City: University of Iowa Press, 1999). See also my book *Impersonations* (Cambridge: Cambridge University Press, 1996), pp. 40–49.

13. Cited in G. P. Akrigg, *Jacobean Pageant* (Cambridge, Mass.: Harvard University Press, 1963), p. 13.

14. *Newes from Scotland*, p. 17.

15. Ibid., p. 15.

16. *Political Works of James I*, ed. C. H. McIlwain (Cambridge, Mass.: Harvard University Press, 1918), p. 272.

17. Ibid., p. 24.

18. From a letter of 5 October 1612, quoted by J. W. Williamson, *The Myth of the Conqueror* (New York: AMS Press, 1978), pp. 138–39.

## Chapter Five: The Pornographic Ideal

1. The fifth and sixth sonnets and woodcuts are missing from the unique exemplar. The book was first published in facsimile in Italian, and subsequently in English as *I Modi The Sixteen Pleasures*, with an introduction and other relevant material, by Lynne Lawner (Evanston: Northwestern University Press, 1988). A more recent, much more detailed and historically informed study of the prints and the woodcut volume is Bette Talvacchia's *Taking Positions* (Princeton: Princeton University Press, 1999), which also has superior reproductions and better translations of the Aretino sonnets, and is the best place to go for a full discussion of both the prints and their place in the Renaissance social and cultural context.

2. See my discussion of a drawing now in Stockholm of Orpheus making love to a youth as an angry maenad watches, "Gendering the Crown," in my collection *The Authentic Shakespeare* (New York and London: Routledge, 2002), pp. 107–28.

3. From the Preface to his translation of Paolo Lomazzo's *Trattato*, *A Tracte containinge the Artes of curious Painting, Caruinge & Buildinge* (Oxford, 1598), p. 6. See my fuller discussion of the subject in my essay "Idols of the Gallery: Becoming a Connoisseur in Renaissance England," in *Early Modern Visual Culture*, eds. Peter Erickson and Clark Hulse (Philadelphia: University of Pennsylvania Press, 2000).

4. David Howarth, *Lord Arundel and his Circle* (New Haven: Yale University Press, 1985), p. 21.

5. The larger issues raised by the statue in relation to the art-historical context are brilliantly elucidated by Leonard Barkan, "Living Sculptures: Ovid, Michelangelo, and *The Winter's Tale*," *ELH* 48 (1981), pp. 639–67. Georgianna Ziegler proposes an alternative source, in English, for the name of Giulio Romano, which presupposes no knowledge at all of his art on Shakespeare's part: "Parents, Daughters, and 'That Rare Italian Master,'" *Shakespeare Quarterly* 36 (1985), pp. 204–12.

6. A mischievous sprite or hobgoblin.

7. The undated painting must have been done at least a decade earlier; but Mrs Kean's petticoats were not an innovation.

## Chapter Six: Imagining Shylock

1. Joseph Hatton, *Henry Irving's Impressions of America* (Boston: Osgood, 1884), p. 231.

2. Coryate, *Crudities* (London, 1611), p. 231.

3. Ibid.

4. Cited by Toby Lelyveld, *Shylock on the Stage* (Cleveland: Western Reserve University Press, 1960), p. 26.

5. From a marginalium transcribed by Frank Marcham, *Lopez the Jew* (Harrow Weald, Middlesex, 1927), n.p.

6. *Copie of a Leter Wryten by a Master of Arte at Cambridge to his friend in London* (1584), p. 80 (reprinted in 1641, and thereafter invariably referred to, as *Leicester's Commonwealth*).

7.  The remarks are cited in Hermann Sinsheimer, *Shylock, The History of a Character or The Myth of the Jew* (London: Victor Gollancz, 1947), p. 66. I am indebted to Charles Edelman, whose study of the case is forthcoming, for the information that the claims are unfounded.

8.  Jay Halio, ed., *The Merchant of Venice* (Oxford: Oxford University Press, 1993), p. 28.

9.  Thomas Wilson, *A Discourse Upon Usury* (London: Bell, 1925), p. 111.

10. James Shapiro, *Shakespeare and the Jews* (New York: Columbia University Press, 1996), p. 27.

11. *Crudities* (London, 1611), p. 231.

12. Shapiro, pp. 55–56.

# Index

Aaron 156
Abbey, Edwin, *Play Scene in Hamlet* 59–60
Achilles 105
Ackerman, Rudolph, *Microcosm of London* 51–3,
    Plate 5
Actors' Workshop, San Francisco 86, 90
Addison, Joseph 54
Admetus 129
Agathon 156
age of consent 98
Alcestis 129
Alcmena 87
Alexander the Great 51
Alleyn, Edward 31–3
Alma-Tadema, Lawrence 139
anachronism 19–24
Anderson, Mary 138–40
Anger, Kenneth 94
Anne of Denmark 103, 111, 119
Antonio, Don (pretender to the Portuguese
    throne) 149
Apollo 117, 120
*Arden of Feversham* 12–13, 41
Aretino, Pietro 112–19, 121, 123, 125
Ariadne 90, 92
Aristophanes 156
Aristotle 9, 24
Armin, Robert 30–1; *Two Maids of Mortlake* 30–1
Arthur, King 105, 108–9
Arundel, Earl and Countess of *see* Howard
Astraea 98–9
Aubrey, John 77

Bacon, Francis 42, 82
Bakst, Leon 142
Barkan, Leonard 166 n. 5.5
Barker, Harley Granville 140–2
Barry, Spranger 45–6
Beaumont, Francis, and John Fletcher 3, 8
Beckett, Samuel 163

Bedford, Lucy Countess of *see* Russell
Bell's Shakespeare 78, 80
Bergeron, David 165 n. 4.12
Bernhardt, Sarah 146
Betterton, Thomas 49, 77, 84, 147
Boccaccio 119
Boel, Cornelius 65
Boydell, John, Shakespeare Gallery 29, 45–53
Brook, Peter 86
buggery 92–4, 96, 115–19
Burbage, Richard 78

Calvin, John 152–3
Camden, William 150
Carmichel, James, *News from Scotland* 100–4
Caracci, Agostino, *L'Aretino* 118
Castiglione 119
Catullus 87, 94
Cecil, Robert 150
Cellini, Benvenuto 122
Chandos portrait 70–83
Chapman, George 68–9
Charles I 121–2
Charles V, Holy Roman Emperor 121
Chaucer, Geoffrey 90, 105
Chesterfield portrait 72–3
Cibber, Colley 50
Circe 96–7
circumcision 155
Clarke, Mary Cowden, *Girlhood of Shakespeare's
    Heroines* 37, 40
clowns 3–4, 20, 30–1, 152
Coleridge, Samuel Taylor 29, 30, 47
Collier, John Payne 83
Columbine 156
*commedia dell'arte* 9, 156–7
Congreve, William 1
Cooke, George Frederick 34
Corneille, Pierre 50
Coryate, Thomas, *Crudities* 148, 154

Covent Garden 19, 38
Craig, Edward Gordon, *King Lear* 63–4
Cromwell, Oliver 154
Cupid and Psyche, Palazzo Tè 123–5, Plate 15

Dance, Nathaniel 34, 36
Davenant, William 49, 50, 76–8, 83
de Beuil, Honorat, Sieur de Racan, *Artenice* 20–1
de Grazia, Margreta 164 n. 3.1
Delacroix, Eugène 56–7, 58
Delarem, Francis 90
Dench, Judi 140
de Vere, Edward, Earl of Oxford 42
Devereux, Robert, Earl of Essex 98, 149–51
de Witt, Johannes 10–12
Diaghilev, Serge 140–2
Diana 89, 97, 98
Dine, Jim 86, Plate 11, Plate 12
Dobson, Michael 165 n.3.1
Doggett, Thomas 144–5
Drayton, Michael, *Poly-Olbion* 68, 109
Droeshout, Martin 65–70, 74, 83, 165 n. 3.2
Drury Lane Theater 51, 129, Plate 5
Dudley, Robert, Earl of Leicester 149
Dulac, Edmund 30, Plate 1

Edelman, Charles 167 n. 6.7
Edmond, Mary 165 n. 3.2
Edward VI 121
Egeus (King of Athens) 95
Eliot, George (Mary Anne Evans), *Daniel Deronda* 155
Elizabeth I 85–6, 89–90, 92, 97–9, 104, 105, 121, 149–50, Plate 13
Elizabeth, Princess, Electress Palatine and later Queen of Bohemia 111
Empson, William 41
English Players' *Hamlet* 58, Plate 7
epithalamia 87
Essex, Earl of *see* Devereux
Euripides, *Alcestis* 129–30
Europa 92
*Everyman* 42

Farnesina Chigi, Rome 143
Farren, Elizabeth 129–30
Flora 125
Florio, John 119

Flower portrait 82–3, Plate 10
Forman, Simon 126–7
Francis I, King of France 121
Frederick, Elector Palatine, later King of Bohemia 111
Fuseli, Henry 34–7, 51, 92–3, 96, Plate 3

Garbo, Greta 94
Garrick, David 32–7, 48, 50, 51, 73, 75, 78, 127–9, 163, Plate 2
Genet, Jean 163
George III 19
George IV 19
Giambologna 121, 122
Goldberg, Jonathan 165 n. 4.12
golden fleece 158
Granville, George, *Jew of Venice* 145, 146
Green, John 31–2, 35
Greene, Robert, *Pandosto* 125
Guarini, G. B., *Pastor Fido* 24, 28

Halio, Jay 151
Harington, Lucy *see* Russell
Harlequin 156
Hancock, John 86, 90
Hanmer, Thomas 133
Harington, Lucy, Countess of Bedford 104–5
Hartley, Elizabeth 129, 131
Harvey, Gabriel 149
Hathaway, Anne 79
Haydocke, Richard 121
Hemminge, William, and Henry Condell 42
Henry V 39
Henry VII 19
Henry VIII 45, 98, 103, 121
Henry Frederick, Prince of Wales 105–11, 121–2
Hercules 90, 105, 129
Hilliard, Nicholas 89
Hippolytus 92
Hogarth, William, *Garrick as Richard III* 32–7, 78, Plate 2
Holbein, Hans 45, 121
Hole, William 21–3, 65
Holland, Peter 86, 88, 92
Hollander, Anne 73
homosexuality 87, 94, 103, 116–18
Howard, Alathea, Countess of Arundel 121
Howard, Leslie 146

Howard, Thomas, Earl of Arundel 121

improvisation 3–4, 9
intermezzi 21
Ireland, William Henry 79–80, *Vortigern* 79, 82, 83
Irving, Henry, *Macbeth* 61–4, *Merchant of Venice* 146–7

James I 97–111, 121
Janssen, Gerard, Shakespeare funeral monument 69–71, 82, Plate 9
Jason 158
Jesse 152
Jesuits 150–1, 153
Jews 144–62
jigs 21
John Bull 19
Jones, Inigo 20–1, 105–9, 121
Jonson, Ben 1, 2, 8, 163; folio titlepage 21–3, 68; poems on Shakespeare 68, 74, 84; portrait 69–70
    *Alchemist* 41
    *Bartholomew Fair* 154
    *Hymenaei* 87
    *Masque of Queens* 104–6
    *New Inn* 2, 8
    *Oberon* 105–11
    *Sejanus* 2, 24
    *Volpone* 24, 26, 41, 119
Josselin, Ralph 155
Jove 87, 92, 123, Plate 14
Judith and Holofernes 98

Kean, Charles 38–40, 56–61, 132, 135
Kean, Mrs Charles (Ellen Tree) 38–40, 58–9, 64, 133–9
Kean, Edmund 146
Kemble, Charles 53–4, 56
Kemble, John Philip, *Hamlet* 47, 49, 56, 132
Kemp, Lindsay 94
Kempe, Will 30
King's Men 2, 8
Knight, G. Wilson 30, 47
Kyd, Thomas, *Spanish Tragedy* 13–14, 15, 56

Laius 111
Lamb, Charles 34, 47
Lee, Sidney 149

Leicester, Earl of *see* Dudley
Leslie, C. R. 133–4, 138
Lopez, Roderigo 149–51, 155
Lord Admiral's Men 151
Lower, M. A. 151

Maia 87
Machiavelli, Niccolo 119
Mackintosh, Charles Rennie 140
Macklin, Charles 145–6, 147–9, 151, 153
Maclise, William, *Play Scene in Hamlet* 58–60
Macready, William 38, 54, 132
maenads 118
Magna Carta 56
Malone, Edmond 42
Manners, Francis, Earl of Rutland 69, 121
Marlowe, Christopher 42
    *Doctor Faustus* 31, 34
    *Jew of Malta* 151
    *Tamburlaine* 31
Marshall, William 65
Mary I 121
Mary Queen of Scots 98, 104
Medea 158
Medusa 87
Meisel, Martin 43, 51
Merchant, W. Moelwyn 51
Michelangelo 122
Middleton, Thomas, *Revenger's Tragedy* 41
—and Thomas Dekker, *Roaring Girl* 41
Miller, Arthur 163
Miller, Jonathan 146
Milton, John 74–6
Minotaur 90, 92, 95–6
Molière, Jean Baptiste Poquelin 50
Montefiore bankers 146
Montrose, Louis Adrian 90
Mortimer, John 78, 81
Moseley, Humphrey 2, 8
Moses 156

Nestor 70
Nijinski, Vaslav 142
*Nobody and Somebody* 31–2, 35
Nossiter, Isabella 45–6
Nunn, Trevor 140

Oedipus 111
Olimpia 123, Plate 14

Olivier, Laurence 146
Orpheus 116, 118
Ovid 97, 122, 125
Oxford, Earl of *see* de Vere

Palazzo Tè, Mantua 117, 120–1, 123, Plate
    14, Plate 15
Palma Giovane 121
Pantalone 156–7
Pasiphaë 92
Peacham, Henry, *Titus Andronicus* sketch 14–15,
    17–18, 21, 43–5, 56
Penthesilea 105
Petrarch 119
Phaedra 92
Phidias 121
Philip II (king of Spain) 149–50
Piper, David 83, 164 n. 3.1
Planché, J. R. 53–7
Plato, *Symposium* 156; 163
Plautus 16
Plutarch 51, 90
Poel, William 56
Pope, Alexander 40, 146, 148
Poussin, Nicholas, *Coriolanus* 51–5, Plate 5
Pritchard, Hannah 127–9, 138
Proserpina 125, 142
Prynne, William 153
Psyche 143; *see also* Cupid
Pugin, A. C. 51, Plate 5

Quin, James, as Coriolanus 51–3

Racan, Sieur de *see* de Beuil
Rachel (Elisa Félix) 146
Racine, Jean 50, 111
Raimondi, Marcantonio 112–14
Rankins, William, *Mirror of Monsters* 95
Raphael 70
Reeve, Ada 146
Reinhardt, Max 94
*Return from Parnassus* 76
Rich, John 19
Richard II 39
Richard III 43
Rizzio, David 104
Robin Goodfellow (Puck) 88
Romano, Giulio 112–43
    *Ceres* 142–3, Plate 16
    *I Modi* 112–19, 125

Rothenstein, Albert 140–2
Rothschild bankers 146
Roubiliac, Louis François 73, 75, 78
Rowe, Nicholas 24, 43–5, 51–5, 90–1,
    127–8
Rowlandson, Thomas 51, Plate 5
Russell, Lucy Harington, Countess of Bedford
    104–6
Rutherston *see* Rothenstein
Rutland, Earl of *see* Manners

Salomon bankers 146
Sant, James 74–6
Sargent, John Singer, *Lady Macbeth* 62–4, Plate 8
Sassoon bankers 146
satyrs 105, 107
Scheie, Danny 94
Schlueter, June 15, 164 n. 1.3
Schoch, Richard, 43, 54, 164 n. 2.1
Schoenbaum, Samuel 83–4
Schuckman, Christian 165 n. 3.2
Serlio, Sebastiano 15–21, 24
Shakespeare, Edmund 41
Shakespeare, Hamnet 41
Shakespeare, William: bad quartos 4; Padua
    folio 4–8; first folio 42, 65–70; portraits
    69–84
    *All's Well That Ends Well* 87
    *As You Like It* 24, 27, 29, 30, 127
    *Comedy of Errors* 156
    *Coriolanus* 51–5, 75
    *Cymbeline* 86, 126, 158
    *Hamlet* 1, 2, 3–4, 24, 30, 37, 41–2, 47–9,
    56, 86, 163, Plate 6, Plate 7
    *Henry IV* 4, 19, 42
    *Henry V* 19, 38–40, 127
    *Henry VIII* 43–5
    *Julius Caesar* 24–5
    *King John* 19, 53–6
    *King Lear* 1, 2, 30, 41, 43, 50, 63–4, 75, 86,
    127
    *Love's Labour's Lost* 2, 86, 152
    *Macbeth* 2, 4–6, 15, 37, 43, 50, 56, 58–9,
    61–4, 75, 126, Plate 3, Plate 4, Plate 8
    *Measure for Measure* 4, 6–8, 15
    *Merchant of Venice* 72, 123–5, 144–63, 152
    *Midsummer Night's Dream* 75, 78, 85–111
    *Much Ado About Nothing* 87, 152
    *Othello* 1, 86, 89, 158

Shakespeare, William continued
    Richard III 19, 32–7, 75, Plate 2
    Romeo and Juliet 2, 29, 45–7, 86, 111, 123, 152
    Tempest 30, 42, 61, 89, 95, 156, Plate 1,
    Titus Andronicus 14–15, 17–18, 21, 43, 156
    Twelfth Night 2, 30, 41, 86, 152
    Winter's Tale 38, 43, 58, 86, 111, 112–43
—and John Fletcher, Cardenio 78–9, 82
Shakespeare Gallery see Boydell
Shakespeare Santa Cruz 94
Shapiro, James 153, 155
Shaw, G. B. 1, 163
Shylock, Christopher 151
Shylock Beauty Salon 151
Shylok, Richard 151
Sidney, Philip 17, 20, 152
slave trade 162
Smirke, Thomas 29
Socrates 70, 156
sodomy see buggery
Soest, Gerard 73–4
Sophocles, Oedipus 9–10, 18–19
Steevens, George 51
Stubbes, Philip, Anatomy of Abuses 96
Swan drawing 10–12

Talma, François Joseph 47, 56–7, Plate 6
Talvacchia, Betty 166 n. 5.1
Tarlton, Richard 30–1
Tasso, Torquato 119
Tate, Nahum 50
Tawney, R. H. 152–3
Taylor, Gary 79
Taylor, Joseph 77–8
Teatro Olimpico, Vicenza 9–10, 18–19, 30
Terence 16
Terry, Ellen 58, 61–4, 133–9, 146
Theobald, Lewis 50, Double Falsehood 78–9, 82, 83

Thespis 21–3
Thurloe, John 155
Titian 121
Titus and Vespasian 15, 17, 164 n. 1.3
Torrigiano, Pietro 121
Tourneur, Cyril, Revenger's Tragedy, see Middleton
tragicomedy 20–2
Tree, Ellen, see Mrs Charles Kean
Tree, Herbert Beerbohm 56
Tuccia 98, Plate 13

usury 152–3

van de Passe, Simon 65
Vasari, Giorgio 112, 122, 125
Vaughan, William 65
Venus Genitrix 142
Virgil 70
Vitruvius 12, 15

Walsingham, Francis 149
Whitehead, William, Roman Father 51, 54
Wilde, Oscar 63–4
Wilson, Benjamin, Garrick as Hamlet 48
Wilson, Thomas, Discourse on Usury 152

Yeomen of the Guard 19

Wallis, Henry, Sculptor's Workshop 82, Plate 9
Warburg bankers 146
Webster, John 2, 8
witchcraft 100–4

Zeuxis 121
Ziegler, Georgianna 166 n. 5.5
Zoffany, Johann, Garrick and Mrs Pritchard in
    Macbeth 45, Elizabeth Farren as Hermione 130,
    Plate 4